The Book
About Marriage

The Book About Marriage

Entering It, Sustaining It, Ending It

Lenard Marlow

Library of Congress Control Number:		2021903776
ISBN:	Hardcover	978-1-6641-6011-8
	Softcover	978-1-6641-6010-1
	eBook	978-1-6641-6009-5

Print information available on the last page.

Rev. date: 02/26/2021

To order additional copies of this book, contact:
Xlibris
844-714-8691
www.Xlibris.com
Orders@Xlibris.com
818140

CONTENTS

Part II
Sustaining the Marriage

Part III
Ending the Marriage

To my grandchildren, Jordon, Jack, Charlie and Camryn

FOREWORD

When I started practicing divorce law in the early 1960s, life was a lot simpler. When we talked about marriage we were talking about a man and a woman and he was called the husband and she the wife. Nor did we have to read their wedding announcement to find out whether she had taken his name or retained her own name. A wife always took her husband's name.

Things are not that simple today. To begin with, a wife does not necessarily take her husband's name. Men and women today marry much later than they did in the 1960s, by which time many women have not only obtained graduate degrees in their maiden names but are also known in their professional or business lives by that name.

It is not that simple for another reason as well. A marriage today is not always between a man and a woman. It can be between two women or two men. Nor has society designated how they are to be referred to. Rather, each couple decides that on their own.

But it is even more complicated than that. Not all couples today who live together in an intimate relationship necessarily marry, and if they don't we refer to their living arrangements as cohabitation. As is the case with those in a same sex marriage, as of yet society has not indicated how they are to be referred to. They decide that for themselves. But unlike a married couple, they do not get divorced when they end their relationship. (They never married.) They just cease co-habiting and go their separate ways.

This variety of living arrangements posed a problem for me. It was not possible to refer to all of these different arrangements separately. Thus, unless I indicate otherwise, I will talk as if they are all marriages between a man and a woman. That will not make what I will say any less relevant for those who are in a different relationship.

PART I

Getting Married

INTRODUCTION

As its title indicates, This is a book about marriage. It is the companion book to another book I wrote entitled *A Common Sense, Practical Guide to Divorce* which, as its title indicates, is about divorce.

This book was originally conceived as a book addressed to someone in a troubled marriage who was struggling with the question of whether they should go forward, get a divorce and end their marriage, or go back, get some professional help and try to sustain it. From my experience working with married couples, I knew that this was a problem that many husbands and wives struggled with for a very long time, often for years. I wrote this book because I felt that I could help them answer that question.

After I began to write the book, I realized that it could also be of value to someone who was not married but who was in a relationship that might lead to marriage. If you are someone in this second group, you are probably not reading this book to answer the question of whether or not you should marry. The fact that you are in love has answered it for you. (As they say, love is the argument that doesn't admit of any argumentation.) Rather, you are only reading it because someone you know told you it was a good book and that you should read it. Nevertheless, I think that it may be of benefit to you as well.

The first reason is that very commonly couples in a relationship that might lead to marriage are also faced with the question of whether they should terminate the relationship or go forward and make it a permanent one. If you are in that second group, and struggling with that question, reading this book may help you make that decision.

The second is that, contrary to what we have been brought up to believe, love and marriage do not, as the famous song says, always go together like a horse and carriage. All too often, when marriage hits a bump in the road, they separate and come apart. My hope is that reading this book will give you a more realistic understanding when it comes to love and marriage and, in doing so, help you to keep them together.

As you will find, the principal theme of this book will be that husbands and wives do not get divorced because of the problems they find in their marriage. They get divorced because of the problems they bring to their marriage. In Part I, I will provide example after example of this. It is my hope that, in reading them, if you are married rather than just in a relationship that might lead to marriage, you will be able to see aspects of your present relationship that the blinding power of the love you experienced, and that so characterizes your relationship before you married, disabled you from seeing, as it disabled the couples I will refer to from seeing.

But the book goes well beyond that. If you are someone who is in a troubled marriage and struggling with the question of which direction to go in, by the time you finishing reading it, you will feel that you are in a position to make that decision. In fact, there will be a short test for you to take that will answer the question for you.

The book will also help you in second way, regardless of which direction you decide to go in. It will provide you with a roadmap that will point you in the right direction.

As I earned over the last 35 years of my career working with couples who had turned for help in an effort to sustain their marriage before they came to me, the sad truth was that, more often than not, the mental health professionals to whom they had turned for help were of no help. They struck out more often than not. Moreover, unlike Babe Ruth, they did not have a lot of home runs to which they could point to correct the imbalance. It was just one strike out after another. Worse, it was not generally understood why that was so.

Part II will explain why and how this happened. In the terms that I will put it, it was because the professionals to whom they had turned for help were following the wrong roadmap. As a result, they were as lost as were the husbands and wives who came to them for help. But Part II will go further. It will provide those of you who have decided to go back in an effort to sustain your marriage with a better roadmap. More important, rather than just selecting the mental health professional you will turn to for help at random, knowing what you will now know, you will only select someone who follows the new roadmap that I will propose.

But suppose that, rather than going back and attempting to address the problems in your marriage, you decide to go forward, get a divorce and end it. If that is the case, how will this book be of help to you? Again, by pointing you in the right direction. Toward that end, Part III will refer you to the companion book that I wrote to this one. It is entitled *A Common Sense, Practical Guide To Divorce*, and you owe it to yourself to read it.

Although husbands and wives do not realize this, they also instinctively follow a roadmap when they decide to divorce. It is the one provided to them by our adversarial legal system. Unfortunately, there is a very serious problem with that roadmap. Moreover, it is not that it won't improve the situation. It is that it will only make matters worse. That, unfortunately, has been the sad legacy bequeathed by our adversarial legal system to all of those who have followed that roadmap. It took what was already a tragedy in their lives and turned it into nightmare.

That companion book will provide you with a better roadmap. And just as there is no other book that will give you the roadmap that this one does when it comes to your marriage, there is no other book that will do the same when it comes to your divorce.

Providing you with those better roadmaps was the intention of both of the books that I have written on the subject. May they be of help to you.

I will close this Introduction by just adding three things. Although this book was not written with couples who were in a sound marriage in mind, I nevertheless believe that it could be of benefit to them as well. The relationship of a couple who has been married for five years or more is not the same as it was when they first married. On the contrary, it is an entirely different relationship. Thus, though they may both still love one another, they are not "in love" with one another as we generally use that term. Put another way, they have a different marriage today than they did when they got married.

First, couples in a sound marriage are more likely to take their relationship for granted. It is not that they no longer appreciate one another. As I said, if they have a sound marriage they undoubtedly still love one another. But they are not necessarily aware of the compromises that they have both made along the way to sustain it. I think that they would have an even better marriage if they were consciously aware of this.

Second. Although I have talked about couples who were in a relationship that might lead to marriage as if they were one group, in reality they are divided into two groups. The first consists of relationships in which one (or both) of the parties is struggling with the question of whether they should terminate the relationship. The second consists of relationships in which one or both of the parties is asking themselves whether they should go forward and make the relationship permanent. However, for the sake of simplicity, I am going to talk as if they constitute one group.

Finally, the fact that I will be referring to so many different people in so many different relationships presented a problem for me. Since what I will say will call into question so much of the conventional wisdom when it comes to marriage and divorce, what I will be presenting will be complex enough as it is without adding to it. Thus, unless I indicate to the contrary, it should be assumed that in every instance I am referring to a marriage between a man and a women.

CHAPTER 1

THE GARDEN OF EDEN

If you want to get the right answer, you will
first have to ask the right question.

As I said in the Introduction, this book is addressed to basically two groups of people. The first consists of people who are not married but who are in a relationship that might lead to marriage. The second consists of couples who are married but who are having serious problems in their marriage. As a result, one or both of them is questioning whether or not they should terminate their marriage. As I said, I believe that a couple who is in a basically sound marriage might also benefit from reading this book, but it is not primarily addressed to couples in that third group.

Part I of the book will be primarily addressed to couples in the first of those two groups. Nevertheless, as I have already indicated, the first of those two groups is often made up of two sub-groups. In the first, one or both of the parties is considering whether they should terminate their relationship. In the second one or both of the parties is considering whether they should go forward and make their relationship more permanent.

Having said that, I must add that Part I will also be addressed to couples who are already married or, in the terms that I have previously put it, have already moved forward and made their relationship more permanent, but where one or both of them is considering terminating their marriage.

The purpose of this book, as I said, is to help those in that second group to make the decision they are struggling with—whether to go forward, get a divorce and end their marriage, or to go back and attempt to successfully work on the problems in it with a view to sustaining it. Moreover, since, if you are in that second group, I am going to give you something that will enable you to decide whether or not it is realistic for you to believe that you will be able to work on the problems in your marriage, you should be able to make that decision by the time you have finished reading the book. That is the better roadmap I referred to in the Introduction. If you are like most husbands and wives, that is the question you have been struggling with for some considerable time. Putting you in a position to make that decision will free you from that conflict. Since the key to that is the new roadmap that I have referred to, I want to tell you how I happened to come up with it.

For more than fifty years of my professional life, I worked with husbands and wives who were in the process of getting a divorce, first as a traditional divorce lawyer and then, for the last thirty-five of those fifty years, as a divorce mediator. In that latter period, I also wrote numerous books addressed to how divorcing husbands and wives who had decided to go forward and end their marriage should do that. In not one of those books had I ever raised the question that I am in this book—whether or not it was realistic for them to believe that they might be able to go back and successfully work on the problems in their marriage.

I never gave any thought to this until I decided to retire, which I did at the end of 2015. One possible reason was that, because I had been so focused on the problems involved in their going forward and ending their marriage, it never occurred to me to address the possibility of their going back and working on the problems in their marriage. But that answer didn't satisfy me and I knew that there had to be more to it than that. Nevertheless, I didn't give very much thought to it.

Ironically, the answer only occurred to me when I began to give thought to writing this book. That is when the many books I had written about divorce proved very helpful to me. What had really been the theme of all of those books? It was that what turned a husband's and wife's divorce into the nightmare that it all too often became was the fact that they made the mistake of following the wrong roadmap, the one bequeathed to them by our adversarial legal system. (In an earlier book, *Common Sense, Legal Sense, and Nonsense About Divorce,* I referred to it as a script. For my present purposes, I felt the metaphor roadmap worked better.) And what was the message in all of the books that I had written? It was that if they wanted to avoid that for themselves, they would have to follow a better roadmap. It was coming to that conclusion that enabled me to write this book.

Though the mental health professionals they had turned to did not realize this, the roadmap they were following had also been bequeathed to them by our adversarial legal system. What was wrong with that roadmap? Its focus was on the wrong place. In my terms, it was causing them to look at the presenting problem rather than at the underlying problem. The presenting problem was the complaint that one or both of them now had when it came to their marriage. The underlying problem, at least from my perspective, was one that the two of them had brought to their marriage. Put another way, my thesis was that the seeds that took root and eventually undermined their marriage were planted a long time ago. They were planted before they got married.

Ironically again, that conclusion was implicit in many of the books that I had previously written, particularly *The Two Roads To Divorce,* and I am going to quote from Chapter 2 of it, entitled "The Garden of Eden."

When something goes wrong, it is natural to look for an explanation. After all, everything must have a cause. The same is true of divorce. There must be a reason. Or, as the law has traditionally put it, someone must be at "fault."

This belief derives from our view of the world, which is grounded in the story of the Garden of Eden. That story tells us that the disharmony that we see everywhere between man and nature is not an inherent part of the human condition or, therefore, inevitable. Rather, what caused Adam and Eve to be expelled from the Garden of Eden (to fall from grace) was human failing (sin).

Our view of marriage and divorce is grounded in the same understanding. Like Adam and Eve, who originally lived in a perfect state of harmony with the world in the Garden of Eden, we believe that husbands and wives did as well. Accordingly, the disharmony that led to their divorce was not an inherent part of their marriage. It was not there "in the beginning." Rather, their falling out of love (the "fall from grace") was caused by the misconduct of one of them. That is what we mean when we say that the divorce was caused by one of the parties–that it was his or her "fault." If one of them had not been guilty of misconduct, they would still have a happy marriage (still be in love). Put simply, marriages do not have to end in divorce. Rather, like the endings of the fairy tales that were read to us as children, we believe that it is possible for husbands and wives to live "happily ever after." Moreover, the harmony in their marriage could still be restored and their marriage saved if the guilty party would only mend his or her ways.

It is understandable that husbands and wives who are locked in an unhappy marriage will view it this way—see themselves as being unhappy because of what the other has done or been unwilling to do. They are too close to what has happened to see it clearly and too emotionally involved in it to look at it objectively. As a result, they feel too much and understand too little. But why do the rest of us, who are able to view their marriage more dispassionately and from more of a distance, not see it any more clearly?

There are a number of reasons for this. The first, as I said, derives from our Garden of Eden cosmology. Since we see their marriage as having been initially perfect, it cannot have been anything that was inherent in their relationship. After all, as everyone who attended their wedding will testify, they were completely in love then, and nothing was out of place. If that is so, it must be something that happened (was introduced into their relationship) later.

The second reason may surprise you. It is that we really do not know why husbands and wives get divorced. Put another way, we do not know any more about why they stop being in love than we do about why they fell in love in the first place. We do not have a clue. And so, even though the two of them are the least reliable witnesses when it comes to their own marriage, we will invariably accept everything they tell us at face value. If they say that their husband or wife was at "fault", and particularly if they give us chapter and verse to support it, we will accept it as gospel. But, then, not having any better explanation, what else can we do?

Unfortunately, being biased observers, the report we will be given will leave out many of the essential ingredients. Put another way, it will tell us what happened, but not why. As a result, it will cause us to make the most common mistake when it comes to divorce. That is to look at the things husbands and wives do and say, and the way in which they act, when

they are unhappy in their marriage, and see that as
the cause of the problem rather than its symptom. It
is to look at the wrong starting point.

What is the right starting point? It is right there in our picture
of the Garden of Eden. It is the snake, which in the context here
represents what each of them brought to the marriage. The snake
was not introduced into the picture at a later point in time—after the
two of them married. The snake was there from the very beginning.
They just didn't see it.

What caused me to see it? Ironically, it was the wedding
announcements in the Styles Section of *The New York Times* that I
had been reading for years. I learned so much about marriage from
them. That is because they gave me a glimpse of what had happened
before the two of them got married. In the terms that I have put it,
they showed me the seeds they had planted that eventually took root
and undermined their marriage. But I will get to that at a later point.

CHAPTER 2

WHOSE FAULT IS IT?

Husbands and wives do not get divorced because they are good people or bad people. They get divorced because they are different people.

Whenever I am asked why husbands and wives divorce, I usually reply, "Because they are desperately unhappy," and leave it at that. Since, at least initially, most divorces are initiated by one person rather than two, it would be more accurate to say it is because one of them is desperately unhappy.

Although the answer I have given is the correct one, it is not the one that those who asked the question expected. They were looking for something more. They wanted to know what took place in the marriage that led to the divorce. If I give them the answer I do, it is because I want to frustrate their tendency to look for simple answers to explain complex problems. It is because I do not want to reinforce their tendency to see the symptom of the problem (the conduct of one of them) as its cause.

Why do we all make this mistake? Again, it derives from our Garden of Eden view of marriage. We see the couple as having started out in a perfect state of harmony—as being at one with one another. We get so taken in by the fact they were in love that we fail to see that there was always a potentially divisive element in their relationship.

We get so taken in by the harmony in the Garden of Eden that we fail to see the snake.

What is it that our Garden of Eden view of marriage prevents us from seeing? It is that, in a very important sense, all matches (marriages) are mismatches. They are made up of two very different people. Worse, brides and grooms are not generally aware of those differences, which accounts for the saying that we marry total strangers. On some level at least, couples may be aware that those differences exist. Nevertheless, the very strong feelings they are experiencing, as well as other factors, will tend to mute their awareness of this. They may even create the illusion there are none, and that the two of them are completely "as one." But, like love itself, that is only an illusion.

Ironically, it is not uncommon that people can now tell you things that took place prior to their marriage, that were tell-tale signs of the problems to come, that they did not see then. (They could not tell you about them now if they did not see them then. They just didn't want to acknowledge them.) There are others who will tell you they realized that they had made a mistake literally from the very beginning of their marriage, or shortly thereafter.

This is a testament to the power of the feelings that so overwhelm our critical faculties. They induce us to hold up pretty pictures for ourselves. They cause us to be taken in by the fairy tale endings portrayed to us on the covers of literally all of our magazines—of Prince Charming awakening Sleeping Beauty. Worse, they disable us from being able to see any of the things that would call them into question.

The problem is that we do not see those feelings as representing a hindrance, let alone a disability. In part, that is because we have been brought up to see the feelings we are experiencing as representing the expression of our highest and noblest aspirations, and what is best in us. But it is also because those feelings fulfill such important needs of ours that they overpower us. They literally carry us away. Unfortunately, having been brought up on fairy tales, no one warns us that they are a potion that will put our critical faculties to sleep.

Even if one of the parties does recognize the potential problems, as they sometimes do, more often than not they will tend to discount them. They will buy into their faith that "love will conquer all" and not give them the attention they deserve. Nevertheless, those differences are there, and they will surface later, when those strong feelings and other factors tend to lose their overpowering force, as they inevitably will. It is then, when they find themselves confronted with the sheer "otherness of the other," that reality will set in.

The differences I am talking about are not differences in interests—that one of them likes to play golf and the other doesn't. While their relationship will obviously be more satisfying if they have common interests, most couples are able to accommodate these differences, even when they are fairly extreme. For example, I have never met a couple who divorced because of differences they had over politics or even religion. Rather, what I am referring to are their different emotional dispositions and, even more important, their different adaptive styles (what might be thought of as their different adaptive strategies)—their different ways of organizing their lives and doing business. In fact, one might say that their marriage is their ongoing act of negotiating and accommodating those stylistic differences. (For the sake of simplicity, I am often going to conflate their different emotional dispositions and adaptive styles and refer to both of them as being the latter.)

Unfortunately, when those different adaptive styles clash, as they so often do, they will lead to serious problems. If the two of them are not able to work out an accommodation between them, they will eventually lead to their divorce. That is because they will not see them as being simply different adaptive styles. Since they will each take for granted their own adaptive style and not see anything unusual or inappropriate in it, the other's adaptive style, which runs such interference with their own, will constitute the problem. Worse, it will appear as a grievous crime. That is because it will make living with the other person difficult if not impossible. Why is that? Because the party who is unhappy in the marriage will not want to change his or her own adaptive style. Nor will they be able to change the other's adaptive style or the effect it is having on them. Not being able to get around it, they will continually run into it. That will be their problem. As I said, it will eventually lead to their divorce.

To be sure, there are exceptions to this—situations in which the problem in the marriage cannot be explained just in terms of the differences in their adaptive styles. For example, there are situations in which one of the parties goes through a sudden, dramatic life change. There are also instances where someone has been guilty of serious misconduct, such as substance abuse or spousal abuse. Even here, however, the relationship between that misconduct and the ultimate divorce is not a simple one, as is witnessed by the fact that rarely does the misconduct lead to an immediate divorce. Rather, the marriage will usually persevere for some time, and even for years, despite the misconduct.

There is another exception as well. Every marriage has a San Andreas fault line running though it—a weak point that will give if too much pressure is applied to it. Generally, husbands and wives are able to dance around that fault line and thereby avoid it. However, certain things can occur which will make that more difficult, if not impossible. That is the case if there has been a very sudden change in their lives, a serious reversal in their fortunes or, worse, a tragedy in their lives, such as the death of a child. It is very difficult for a marriage to survive the death of a child. A tragedy of this magnitude will expose the fault line, put too much pressure on it, and it will give.

Nevertheless, these are the exception rather than the rule. In most instances, the friction is caused by the ordinary, not the extraordinary. The proof of this is the fact that it is not uncommon for husbands and wives to divorce one another for the very reason that they married one another. What was once the mighty glue that held the relationship together has now become the acid that is eating it away. When I mention this to couples who have been married for a relatively short period of time, I commonly get a smile of recognition from one of them—usually the one initiating the divorce. If I do not get the same smile from those who have been married for a longer period of time, it is not because it is any less true. It is just that so much has happened, and so much hurt has built up over the years of their marriage, they are no longer able to see this.

Let me give you an example of this. In the early years of my practice, when I was still an adversarial divorce lawyer, a woman who had married when she was very young consulted with me. She had literally gone from her father's home to her husband's home. "What attracted you to your husband when you first met him?" I asked her. "He knew where he was going. He was able to take charge. He got things done," she replied. It was not difficult to understand how someone who had always been dependent on someone else could have been attracted by those traits. But that was seventeen years ago. Things were different now. She was older. Her view of herself had changed. She was also less dependent. "What is the problem now?" I asked again. "It always has to be his way. He never takes into consideration how I feel. He is a bully." She was divorcing him for the very reason she had married him.

There is something else that contributes to the problem. That is how husbands and wives act when the other's adaptive style begins to become more prominent and they become unhappy in their marriage. It is also how they will each view the other's actions and, in turn, what their reaction will be. That is what I referred to earlier as the mistake of confusing the symptom of the problem with its cause. Unfortunately, this will only add further weight to what is already an overburdened relationship. Not being able to see their own role in any of this—how their conduct contributed to what has happened—their husband's or wife's inappropriate conduct will seem to be without justification, or at least without adequate justification. Moreover, it will become the focus of all of their attention and generate feelings that will fuel reactive conduct on their part and, in turn, on the part of their husband or wife. It will become a viscous cycle. That is always what happens in unhappy marriages. In time, as these actions and reactions play themselves out, husbands and wives no longer find themselves relating to the person they thought they married. Rather, they find themselves relating to a very different person.

Let me give an example of this. A man who originally thought he had married a very organized woman now finds that he is married to a wife who is compulsive, not organized. In time, the husband who related in an appropriate manner to his wife who he thought was organized, begins to relate very differently to his wife who he now feels is compulsive. In fact, as his irritation over her compulsiveness increases, he begins to pick on her for no reason at all, or to pick on her excessively even when he does have a reason. Unfortunately, his wife, who happens to be a bit compulsive, now finds herself married, not to the nice man who she thought she had married, but to a husband who picks on her for no reason at all, or at least for no apparent reason. Since she cannot understand why he is picking on her, and in the hope that this will assuage his upset, she responds by trying to show increased affection towards him. However, because he is angry with her, her husband does not respond to her demonstrations of affection as she would like and even rebuffs them. Since his wife does not understand why her good intentions have been ignored and rebuffed, she is understandably hurt and upset. Nor is her husband entirely unmindful of this since, underneath his irritation, he is basically a decent person. Nevertheless, because of his own upset and consequent anger, he has a very limited ability to respond to his wife's overtures which, on one level at least, anger him (because they do not address the underlying problem), but which, on another level, also leave him feeling somewhat guilty (because his wife does not know why her kindness is being repaid in that manner). In short, in time each of them is living out a very different marriage to a very different husband and wife than the one they married.

There is a moral in this. It is that our misunderstanding of how it is and why it is that marriages end in divorce causes us to respond inappropriately. It leads us to make judgments. Judgments may be appropriate in the face of a crime. They are not, however, when what we are confronted with is a tragedy. In those instances, silence, the suspension of judgments, is the more appropriate response. And let there be no mistake, divorce is a tragedy.

CHAPTER 3

A CROSSROAD

You are not lost. You just don't know where you are.

As I said earlier, you are at a crossroad and you have to decide how you are going to proceed. You can either go forward or you can go back.

To go forward means to conclude that there is no future in your marriage and to proceed to get a divorce. To go back means to decide that you are not prepared to do that and to explore the possibility that you may still be able to work on the problems in your marriage. Obviously, I cannot make that decision for you. But I would like to help you make it for yourself. I am going to start by addressing the second of those two choices, namely, going back and attempting to work on the problems in your marriage. I will then address the problems involved in going forward and ending it.

As you will find, there are problems either way. If that is the case, why am I going to start by exploring the possibility of going back? Because you will not solve your problems by going forward. All that you will do is exchange one set of problems for another—a set of known problems for a set of unknown problems. If you are extremely unhappy in your marriage and want to end it, you will admittedly not see it that way. Since your problem is your marriage, it is natural to assume that if you end your marriage you will end your problem as well. Unfortunately, it is not that simple. Consider the situation.

If you decide to go forward and end your marriage it is not because you intend to retire from life and enter a convent or monastery. Rather, if you are like most people, you are going to go on with your life, form a new relationship, and eventually remarry. That is what divorcing husbands and wives generally do.

But those new relationships are not problem free. How could they be if as many or more second marriages end in divorce as do first marriages? You just don't know what those problems are going to be. But it is not hard to imagine them. Now, all that you have to deal with is your husband or wife and, if you have any, your children. We will call that two-dimensional chess. If you go forward, however, it is going to get more complicated. There may well be your former husband's or wife's future spouse or significant other, his or her children, and their relationship with your children. And, in the background at least, there will be all of the other players in the drama—their former husbands and wives, your former in-laws, etc., all of whom will necessarily interact in the drama. In short, in terms of difficulty, it will be like going from two dimensional chess to three dimensional chess. To be sure, you may not see any of this as a problem, unless your life has already moved on. But, as is the case with your present marriage, the fact that you didn't see it coming doesn't mean that it wasn't waiting to happen.

That is why it is always better to start with the problems you have. As I said, you know what they are. But even if, because you have already embarked on a new relationship—which is so common today—you do know the problems that you will inherit if you go forward, there is always the danger that, being afraid that you will lose the opportunity if you do not grab it, you will underestimate them. After all, you did that when it came to your present marriage. Why would you think that you won't do the same thing again?

There is another reason why you should start with the question whether it makes sense to attempt to go back and work on the problems in the marriage, and this applies to those who have already made the firm decision to go forward and end the marriage. As I said, the purpose of the new roadmap I am going to propose is to put you in the position of being able to make a determination as to whether or not it is realistic to believe that, if you go back and work on the problems in your marriage, you will be left with a marriage that meets your essential needs. That is the purpose of the assessment that you will make when you get through reading this book. That is not a question that your present roadmap asks. It couldn't. It doesn't have the means to answer it, which is why your efforts up till this point have been so unsuccessful. As I said, the focus of the roadmap you have been using is on the wrong place. Its focus is on the symptoms of your problems, not at their cause.

That is why the roadmap I am going to propose, and the assessment that you are going to make on the basis of it, will be of value to you even if you have already made the firm decision to go forward and end your marriage. It will help you validate that decision, thereby hopefully removing any lingering doubts you may have. Your present roadmap cannot do that. As I said, it doesn't ask that question and couldn't answer it even if it did. That is why so many husbands and wives are left struggling with the decision of whether they should go forward or whether they should go back.

CHAPTER 4

A BETTER ROADMAP

*If you want to get from where you are to where you want to be,
you will have to follow the right roadmap.*

I said that my experience was that far too many couples who had sought professional help with the problems in their marriage did not get the help they needed and were looking for, as a result of which their situation did not improve and they ended up getting divorced. I then suggested that the reason for this was that, in the terms that I put it, the mental health professionals to whom they turned for help were following the wrong roadmap. It didn't give them an accurate picture of where they were (really how they had gotten to where they were) or, therefore, what they had to do to get from where they were to where they wanted to be. Having followed the wrong roadmap, they were just as lost when they got through as they had been when they began.

I now want to revise that statement just a bit. Rather than talking in terms of being "the reason," I would prefer to say that "one of the reasons" for this was that they were given the wrong roadmap. That will hopefully avoid the danger of suggesting that all marriages are cast in the exact same mold. I am not suggesting that. I am only saying that, notwithstanding their differences, there are very strong family resemblances in all marriages. My use of the metaphor of a roadmap will hopefully reinforce that understanding.

There is another reason to employ the metaphor of a roadmap. As will be clear when I contrast the two roadmaps, the one we have used up until this point and the one that I am going to propose we substitute in its place, they cause us to ask very different questions. In the terms that I will put it, the roadmap that married couples have been given up until this point caused them to ask the wrong question, which is why they did not get a satisfactory answer. Thus, if they want a better (more satisfactory) answer, they will first have to ask a better question. To do that they will need a new roadmap.

What is the roadmap that they have used up until this point? As I characterized it, it is one that reflects a Garden of Eden cosmology. It is one that says that the two of them started out in a state of perfect harmony. As I said earlier, everyone who was at their wedding will testify that they were completely in love then, and that nothing was out of place. That necessarily leads to the question, what happened to disrupt that state of perfect harmony? In the terms here, the Garden of Eden cosmology embodied in the roadmap they were using provided the answer. The harmony was disrupted by the misconduct of one of them following their marriage. Put another way, if he or she had not been guilty of such misconduct, they would still be in a state of perfect harmony.

What is wrong with that roadmap? It is based on a fantasy. The two of them did not start out in a state of perfect harmony. How could they have when all matches (marriages) are mismatches? They simply did not realize this at the time. The powerful feelings that they were experiencing, and that all of those who attended their wedding witnessed, just disabled them from being able to see this. As I said, there were telltale signs of the inherent disharmony in their relationship even then. They just didn't want to see them.

I said that the significance of the different roadmaps we could employ when it comes to the problems husbands and wives find themselves faced with in their marriage was that, based on their understanding and characterization of their problems, they encourage us to ask different questions. In terms of the roadmap that we inherited from our adversarial legal system, the question it encouraged us to ask was, whose fault was it?

What question will we be encouraged to ask based on the roadmap that I am proposing we should substitute in its place? Since that roadmap sees their relationship as always having been in a state of balanced-imbalance, which could have been upset at any time, the question that it will encourage us to ask is not why are they getting divorced, but why are they getting divorced now. Why didn't they get divorced two years ago, when the wife first raised the question in her mind? Why aren't they getting a divorce two years from now, when their youngest child will graduate from high school. After all, as I said earlier, the problem was not introduced after they got married, as our present roadmap suggests. It was there right from the beginning. Put another way, it was always there. And since it was always there, it could have undermined their marriage at any time. It just happened to do so now.

CHAPTER 5

WHAT DOES IT MEANS TO SAY I LOVE YOU?

Love is the argument that admits of no argumentation.

Before I proceed, I need to take a short excursus. People who marry do so because they are in love. This is not to say that other considerations do not enter into their decision. They most certainly do. But there were no end of other people who possessed the necessary qualifications to satisfy those other considerations. In fact, both parties had no doubt had relationships with someone else before this one where that was the case. But they were not in love with that person or, if they were, there were other considerations that caused that relationship to end. But they are in love now and, but for that, they would not be getting married. That is because love is the basis for what we refer to as romantic marriage and, though that was not always the case, for most people today romantic love is the precondition for marriage. And that was the case here. As I said, everyone who attended their wedding would testify to that.

That raises a question. What does it mean to say that you are in love with someone? More important for our present purposes, what are you saying when you tell someone, "I love you"?

Based on the canons of romantic love, to say to someone that you love them is to express your attitude toward them. It is to pay them a compliment. In fact, it is to pay them the highest compliment that you can. It is to say that they are special, they are wonderful, they are beautiful. It is to adore them and put them on a pedestal. In short, when someone declares that he or she is in love, it has nothing to do with them. It is all about the object of their love. At least that is according to the cannon of romantic love.

Nothing could be further from the truth. Although the person receiving the complement is not aware of this, the person paying him or her the compliment is not really saying anything about them. They are saying how the object of their love is making them feel about themselves. They have never felt so alive and so at one with themselves in their lives as they feel now (unless they have been in love before) and they want to continue to feel that way. That being the case, they want to do whatever they can to maintain those feelings, and the fact that the object of their love is experiencing the same feelings that they are serves to reinforce this.

That is the good news. Unfortunately, as we will shortly see, there is bad news as well. The fact that their being in love is having the effect on them that it does will all too often result in their not seeing, or not taking into account even if they do, the tell-tale signs that are sending a signal to them that there may be trouble ahead if they proceed and act on those feelings. In the terms that I have put it, in keeping with the Garden of Eden cosmology that we are endorsing, what they do not see or therefore take into account is the snake.

CHAPTER 6

YOU GET WHAT YOU SEE

If we don't see it, it is because we don't want to see it.

I said earlier that so much of what I know about marriage I learned by reading the wedding announcements in the Styles Section of *The New York Times*. It was somewhat a sociological study over time.

They were very different in the early 1960's when the changes that most bear on what concerns me first began to appear. To begin with, they were very brief, providing little more than name, rank and serial number. The announcement always featured a formal picture of the bride, but not necessarily one of the groom. If the announcement was in *The New York Times*, the bride had probably attended college and perhaps even graduated from college, though the degree that she had gone to college to get was really an Mrs. degree. Thus, the announcement did not say very much about her. But, given her age (in most cases she would have been no more than in her early 20's) there was not very much to say.

The wedding announcement said a bit more about the groom, however, who was in his mid to late 20's, or perhaps even older. He would not only have graduated from college, but in most instances from a fine one. He would also have either gone on to graduate school or started a career in the business world. In fact, from the standpoint of the bride's family, who had put the announcement in the paper, it was to show what a good catch their daughter had made.

Looking back, there were also other things that distinguished it from wedding announcements today. To begin with, the groom was usually at least five years older than the bride. Today, one third of the time, either the difference in their ages is only one or two years or the wife is actually older than her husband. In any event, it is the rare case where the bride will not be at least 27 or 28. Like the groom, as often as not she will be in her early to mid 30s.

In the past, it was very unlikely that either of the parties had been married before. The same is not true today. Again, in the past the wife always took her husband's name. Today she may or may not. Marrying much later, she will often have already established a separate professional or career life for herself using her maiden name. Even if that is not the case, many women today want to maintain their separate identities.

In the past, the ceremony was invariably performed by an ordained clergyman. Today it is often performed by a friend or relative of one of the parties who was ordained as a "universal life minister" for that purpose. Even if it is officiated by an ordained clergyman, given the fact that the couple will often come from different religious backgrounds, the person performing the ceremony will sometimes be "assisted" by a second clergyman. And, of course, the picture today will be of the two of them, not just the bride. And it will be a very informal one, not a formal one.

While the differences in the announcements were revealing and taught me a great deal about the changes that had taken place in marriage in the second half of the 20th century, they were not the primary reason why I read them. There was another significant change in them. In an effort to make them more interesting, they became more personalized. They told a story about how the two of them met and the history of their relationship as told by the couple, who had submitted the information to The New York Times that would later be used for the announcement. But though the couple did not realize it, it told a great deal more. In my terms, the story they told made me come to realize that the seeds that would take root and grow into the problems that would later undermine their marriage were planted prior to their marriage and not, as our Garden of Eden cosmology would have us believe, introduced into the marriage at a later point in time. In many instances it even indicated just what those problems would be.

With that in mind, I am going to relate a story that appeared in the Styles Section of *The New York Times*. I want to acknowledge in advance that it is very unusual and, as such, just as revealing. That is the whole point of the story. As revealing as it is, the participants did not see it as that. If they had, one or both of them would have called off their wedding. But they didn't do that.

The wife was 33 and the groom 32. They both grew up on Manhattan's Upper East Side, but moved in very different social circles. She was an alpha girl. "She's always been the leader of the pack" a friend said. When she first met him at an engagement party, she thought he was a "weird nerd." The impression didn't change when he moved next door to her parents' apartment several years later. But she softened when he wrote her a sensitive condolence note after her father died, and invited him to a party, following which they began dating.

Their wedding announcement described their relationship as follows: "In some ways, they are complete opposites. She loves Jimmy Choo heels and parties that are reported in Women's Wear Daily. He likes conservative clothes (a spread collar shirt is radical) and evenings spent watching sports on TV."

"He had—I've never heard of this— a *Super Bowl* party," 'Ms. . . . said'."

"When they moved in together, Ms. . . . took down his Bruce Springsteen and Tom Seaver posters. 'She made me put in closets and shoe stuff' Mr. . . . said with a scowl."

"There was a regrettable incident at Gucci when she tried to buy him loafers." 'I'm a lawyer', he protested. 'They are so alien to me'."

"But they are also ideal foils for each other. Mr. . . . is down to earth, quick on his feet and just as feisty as Ms. . . . The couple trade repartee that if not out of Noel Coward, is at least reminiscent of the romantic tension of 'Friends'."

"If I don't brush my teeth", 'Ms. . . . said,' "he puts my toothbrush on my pillow with toothpaste."

"Not with toothpaste," 'Mr. . . . corrected.' "It would spoil the pillow."

It is not irrelevant that the announcement included the fact that the bride was attended by 13 bridesmaids, "wore a made-to-order Carolina Herrera ivory gown," and that the wedding was held at Mar-a-Lago in Palm Beach, which was described as "a Moorish fantasy in gilt, marble and tile, as flat-out gaudy as anything Mr. Trump built from the ground up."

Needless to say, this story raises a lot questions. You didn't need to have a PhD in psychology to know that this marriage was not going to last. But why did it take place at all? I will get to that at a later point. For the time being I just want to say that this marriage represents a classic example of what I suggested earlier, namely, that husbands and wives commonly divorce one another for the very reason they married one another.

There is a tendency to explain this in another way. It is to say that opposites attract. I am not saying that. I don't believe that to be true. If opposites attract one another, how do we explain the fact that they repel one another as well?, which is certainly what was going to happen here. No, the more interesting question is why future husbands and wives do not see these glaring differences (problems) when they are staring them right in the face?

It will be objected that the husband and wife here were just so extreme and so atypical, to the point of being little more than a caricature, that they could not possibly be used to support any conclusion that could apply to any other married couple. However, this criticism misses the point. Yes, the husband and wife here were extreme opposites. They didn't seem to have a single thing in common. They seemed to be at variance at every point. Nor were they unaware of this. Yet that still didn't cause them to take stock of the situation and question whether or not they should go ahead and get married.

But, as the announcements in the Styles Section of *The New York Times* make clear, the same is true of your more typical husband and wife. I will just quote from three other announcements to make my point. I could have quoted from twenty more.

"'I'm organized to a fault', Mr. . . . said. She's a tornado of clothes flying out of the closet, always missing one shoe. I tend to be more of a skeptic, a dark cloud, and she has a wonderful, insuppressible optimism. I try to borrow a bit of that from her, but I don't think she wants to borrow any of my organizational skills'."

––––––––––––

"Were opposites. He's meticulous and thinks things through, which is probably very good for me. He's the calming force in our lives."

––––––––––––

The wife, who was 40 years or age and was keeping her name, was a senior staff lawyer for the American Civil Liberties Union. This was her first marriage. She had graduated summa cum laude from Columbia. She also had a master's degree from Princeton and a law degree from Yale, and following her graduation from law school had clerked for an Associate Justice of the United States Court of Appeals for the Second Circuit. The Husband, who had been married previously, was 42 years of age and was a freelance film and visual-effects producer. He graduated from Emerson College.

The two of them met on a dating service. "I liked that he lived in Brooklyn and that he had been on a safari, as I had," Ms. . . . said. "He also enjoyed 'The Daily Show,' which made me think he might be a witty person who appreciated incisive political commentary."

"On a June afternoon, they got together for coffee at a Manhattan cafe, and chatted for 30 minutes." 'I loved his adventurous spirit,' she said. 'He had traveled throughout Europe and to South America and Southeast Asia. I wasn't meeting many guys from Brooklyn who could share these kinds of experiences'."

"Mr. . . . was equally impressed." 'I was struck by the fact that she was working so hard to bring racial justice to the world,' he said." 'She was more than just a beautiful woman; she was a very intelligent person who was very up on current events'."

"The next month, they met at a Manhattan restaurant for their first date, and talked about topics like work, their love of travel and their cultural and religious background (she is from a Bengali Muslim family and he is Roman Catholic). They also bonded over the shared pain of losing a father . . . 'He was so empathetic, so warm and engaging' Ms. . . . said'."

"They began dating and soon found that they did not share all things in common. He worked in television; she did not own a television set. He preferred quiet evenings at home with family; she liked the theater and fine restaurants. 'In some ways we were total opposites,' Ms. . . . said", 'but that's O.K. because when we fell in love with each other, we also fell in love with our differences'."

I am going to have to return to this story since it bears on so many issues that I will bring up at a later point—their different religious backgrounds, their different educational backgrounds, the fact that they do not have as many interests in common as they first thought they did. For the time being, I just want to use this story to underscore what I have been arguing up to this point, namely, that the seeds that will take root and grow into the problems that may later undermine their marriage were planted prior to their marriage, not afterwards.

The couple in the first story I related saw that there were these extreme differences but ignored them. The couple in this last story saw them as well, but romanticized them away. But those differences may come back to haunt them when the romantic haze that clouds their ability to see them for what they are dissipates, as it inevitably will. For the time being, I just want to underscore that it is not the fact that they do not share all things in common that may create a problem for them in the future—that one of them likes coffee and the other tea. Those are just differences in taste. What we are talking about here are differences in adaptive styles—how we each relate to the world. Differences in taste are compatible with any and all adaptive styles. But different styles are not necessarily compatible with one another.

The wife in this last story acknowledged that when she said that the two of them were "total opposites." We don't say that we are total opposites because one of us likes coffee and the other likes tea. We just say that our tastes are different. In other words, what the wife here was referring to, but then romanticized away, goes much deeper. And if their different adaptive styles are as different as she suggests—if the two of them are "total opposites"—those are the seeds that they have planted that are likely to come back and haunt them in the future.

CHAPTER 7

YOU ALSO GET WHAT YOU DON'T SEE

Appearances can be deceiving.

I want to relate another story. This was not one reported in the Styles Section of *The New York Times*. It involved the daughter of a good friend of mine, who I had known since she was a little girl.

My friend's daughter had a tendency to be somewhat anxious. She tended to rush out and greet problems before they arrived. Following her marriage, I asked her whether her husband knew just how anxious she was before they got married. "No," she replied, "I wanted him to like me." (For his part, her husband had a tendency to be somewhat laid back. Unopened bills could sit in his desk draw for weeks. He didn't advertise that fact about himself either.) These character traits or, as I characterized them, adaptive styles, were what each of them brought to the marriage that the other was going to have to live with. Nor would it be any defense that they hadn't seen them or been told about them in advance. They were going to have to live with them anyway.

Was my friend's daughter being deceptive here? No. There wasn't a deceptive bone in her body. In fact, she was one of the nicest, healthiest persons I knew. She was just putting her best foot forward, and her being anxious was not her best foot.

I made a prediction when it came to the first marriage in the previous chapter (where the wife's initial reaction to her husband was that he was a "weird nerd"). It was going to end in divorce. Would I make the same prediction when it came to this marriage? No. To be sure, given the incredible number of variables at play, it is impossible to make predictions in other people's lives. Nevertheless, if I had to here, it would be that this marriage would go the distance. Ironically, I would base my prediction on the very deception that the wife here engaged in that many people might find somewhat off-putting.

Let me explain. Neither of the parties in the first marriage in the previous chapter thought there was anything unusual or out of place in their conduct. On the contrary, they thought it was perfectly normal and appropriate for them to act and react as they did. More to the point, even if they had been told that there was something unusual or out of place in their conduct, there was nothing they could have or would have wanted to do about it. Whether we characterize it as their emotional dispositions or their adaptive styles, it was who they were.

The wife in the story that I have just related was different. At least to some extent, she knew that her anxiety was a problem. More important, she was able and willing to adapt to the demands of the situation—as we would say, to make compromise with life—rather than allow it to prevent her from achieving what was important to her. In fact, that was a sign of her health. To be sure, the very different adaptive styles that she and her husband each brought to the marriage were going to be an ongoing problem in their marriage. But, as the wife (and her husband) had already demonstrated, in the name of the benefits she felt she derived from the relationship, she was able and willing to make some accommodation to prevent the problem that they represented from getting out of hand.

CHAPTER 8

TROUBLE

*If you didn't see it coming, that is because
you weren't paying attention.*

I now want to relate another story. Like the stories in Chapter 6, the announcement of this couple's marriage appeared in the Styles Section of *The New York Times*. It read in part as follows:

"After dating for a year, they began a series of in-depth conversations about creating a successful marriage. So in-depth that Mr. . . ., not wanting to overlook a single topic, put together a 37 page report and conversation guide. His questions, discussed for eight hours over a four-day period, included subjects like finances, religion, family and children."

"I thought, 'Wow, I had never heard of anything like that'," Ms. . . . said." 'But I appreciated the fact that he was trying to establish a solid foundation, and at the end of those conversations, we both knew we wanted to get married'."

Needless to say, there were a lot of other reactions the wife here could have had. There were also a lot of questions she could have asked herself that she didn't, including "What kind of person would go to the trouble that he did in order to create a report and conversation guide such as this and then take the time to go through it in such depth?" Second, and more important, "Do I want to be married to such a person?"

How do you explain this? I will address that at a later point. For the time being, I just want to dispel the suggestion that the explanation could be in the fact that they were young, lacking in intelligence, or inexperienced. To be sure, they weren't old. But they weren't young either. They were both 32. Again, by any standard, they had sufficient intelligence. She graduated magna cum laude from Washington University in St. Louis and received her M. B. A. from Harvard. He graduated from Harvard and received his M.B.A. and a master's degree in education from Stanford. Nor were they neophytes in the world itself. She was a senior investment director at Cambridge Associates, an investment advisory firm. He was a senior product manager at the research division of Capital One.

With so much going for them, how did both of them (but she really more than he) miss it such big time? I will address that a little further on. Before I do that, however, I want to make another, equally disturbing observation here.

On the face of it, the in-depth conversations they engaged in, together with the 37 page report and conversation guide that accompanied it, were for the purpose of determining whether or not they had the basis for a successful marriage—whether their interests and goals were in sync—-whether they held similar views when it came to "finances, religion, family and children?" But was that really its purpose? Consider the issue of religion. The two of them had been dating for about a year. It has to be assumed that in that time the husband had learned about the wife's preferences when it came to food—that she liked Italian food but didn't like Indian food. How did he learn that? By putting together a report and conversation guide? No. By going out to dinner with her, which they had done countless times over the period in question. Was it any different when it came to her attitude toward religion? Hadn't he had more than a sufficient opportunity to learn that as well?

But what about children? They didn't have any, so how were they going to learn about one another's attitudes here? Again, not from the report and conversation guide that the husband had put together. We all know how they answered the questions there. It was going to be nothing but vacuous platitudes—-"I love children. I think children are the most important thing in a marriage." But did that tell them who was going to change their diapers, take them to school, or do their homework with them? Of course not.

If I am right in saying that this was not the real purpose of the husband's report and conversation guide, what was its purpose? It had to have a purpose. After all, the husband had invested a tremendous amount of time and effort in preparing it, not to mention the 8 hours the two of them spent going over it in that four-day period.

While this is not very flattering when it comes to the husband, his real purpose in preparing this report and conversation guide was to establish the rules that would define their marriage. You might say that this was his insurance policy. He had written the script and it has to be assumed that he also directed the performance. In going over the 37 page report, he let the wife know what he expected and, since it was expressed in vague and lofty abstractions, she indicated her agreement, which it has to be assumed he wrote down in the report. It was all there in black and white. Thus, if the wife later deviated from his expectations, he would always be able to hold her to the line by calling her attention to the fact that he was not asking anything of her that she had not already agreed to.

But he was doing something more, or at least trying to. He was establishing who had the right to make the rules. To be sure, he was not likely to succeed on either account, but that was what he was trying to do nevertheless.

Again, why did the wife not see any of this. It was not for lack of intelligence or experience. That is why I emphasized their educational and work related backgrounds. If this had come up during the course of her work, the wife would never have missed all of the telltale signs here. Rather, she would have questioned what the husband was trying to do. Why did she miss all of those signs here? Because there was a very powerful force at play here that was preventing her from seeing them. I have already referred to it.

I made a prediction as to the likely outcome of the first marriage that I related in Chapter 6 (where the wife's initial reaction to her husband was that he was a "weird nerd") and the marriage that I related in Chapter 7 (where the wife was somewhat anxious). What would be my prediction here? Since everything points to trouble ahead, I would have to say that there was a good chance that they would end up getting a divorce. Why just a "good chance" rather than "necessarily"? It was what I concluded was the husband's real purpose in preparing this report and conversation guide. As I characterized it, it was his insurance policy. Insurance against what? Against the possibility that his wife might turn out to be different than he expected. That was what he was trying to protect himself against. But if he later found that his fears were not justified (and there was nothing that I read in their wedding announcement that suggested they were), he might realize that he didn't need this insurance policy and it would never be heard of again.

CHAPTER 9
DIFFERENCES

Not all differences make a difference. Not all problems create problems.

As I indicated previously, my prediction when it came to the first marriage that I related in Chapter 6 was that they would end up getting divorced. I very much doubt that the couple in the story that I related in Chapter 7 (where the wife was somewhat anxious) will. There were two reasons for this. The first is that the first couple literally had nothing in common. They were polar opposites. I was not surprised that the wife was at first repelled by her husband, and rejected him as a "weird nerd." What surprised me was that she ever changed her opinion. The same was not true of the couple in Chapter 7. They had everything in common. They just had different adaptive styles.

They were also very decent people and very much liked one another. I know that because I know them. I am sure that the wife here can drive her husband a little crazy from time to time, but I also know that he will tell you that she is the nicest person he knows. It is hard to believe that the couple in the first story that I related in Chapter 6 will feel the same way they did when they got married for very long. It is not hard to believe that the couple in the story I related in Chapter 7 will continue to feel the same way.

While it is true that husbands and wives who have different adaptive styles may get divorced over this, it doesn't follow that they necessarily will. It depends upon all of the other factors at play. While there are inevitably considerations that will necessarily undermine their marriage, there are also considerations that will hold their marriage together. Not every problem is a problem.

One of the things that has always struck me is the fact that, as I put it, husbands and wives are invariably cut from the same cloth. Having said that, I have to add that in many ways husbands and wives are not cut from the same cloth, and this is true whether they are of the same sex or opposite sexes. However, since this is a very complicated (and admittedly controversial) issue, I want to postpone a discussion of it to Part II. In the meantime, and if you have difficulty with what I have just suggested, I will ask you to give me the benefit of the doubt until I have had an opportunity to address this in more detail. For the time being, I want to focus on where husbands and wives, whether they are of the same sex or opposite sexes, are the same rather than different.

When I address the fact that they are different, I will not be talking about their being different in the sense that any two people are different. I will be talking about their being different because men and women are different—in the terms that I have put it, that they are not cut from the same cloth.

The fact that, in one sense, husbands and wives are cut from the same cloth was certainly true of the couple in the first story. Their adaptive styles may have been polar opposites, but that didn't mean that they weren't cut from the same cloth. They clearly were.

One example of this is the similarity in a husband's and wife's basic intelligence. I am not talking about education. I am talking about basic intelligence. In the early 1900's it was not anywhere as common for women to go to college as it is today. But that didn't mean that they weren't as intelligent as their husbands. (While my father went both to college and graduate school, my mother, who came from a more affluent family, barely completed one year of college. But she was every bit as smart as my father.)

Today it can be just the opposite. She may have both a college degree and a graduate degree and he only have completed high school. But that doesn't mean that he is not as smart as she is. That is why I went to the lengths that I did to indicate the educational backgrounds of the husband and wife in the last marriage that I related in Chapter 6 (where the wife had degrees from Columbia, Princeton and Yale and the husband had a degree from Emerson). By any conventional standard she would be considered more "educated" than he was. Would I make a prediction that, on the basis of that difference, they are likely to get a divorce? Absolutely not.

I am not saying that a husband's and wife's intelligence is exactly the same. I am just saying that they are both on the same page. I have worked with literally thousands of husbands and wives who were in the process of getting a divorce. I think that I could count on the fingers of one hand the number of times that the difference in their intelligence was so great that I found myself wondering how she could have married him or how he could have married her. On the contrary, the thing that has always impressed me the most is the fact that, when it comes to intelligence, husbands and wives are invariably cut from the same cloth.

In that regard it is important to remember that not all differences make a difference. No husband or wife ever got divorced because one of them liked coffee and the other liked tea—what I previously characterized as differences in taste. Nor will they get divorced because she likes to go to concerts and he doesn't, or because he likes to go to ball games and she doesn't. Differences only become a problem in one of two instances, first, when it doesn't leave them with enough in common and, second, if it is a problem for the other person and the other person is unable or unwilling (and it usually boils down to the same thing) to make accommodations with respect to it. If a wife yells at her husband every time he goes to a ball game, his going to ball games is going to become a problem. If she just makes different arrangements for herself when he does that (she goes out to lunch or to a museum with one of her girlfriends), it won't become a problem. As a general rule, what I am calling a difference in the second sense is only likely to become a problem if the difference is directed at the other party. A wife's going to concerts is not directed at her husband. Her being anxious is, because she is going to want him to be as anxious about the perceived problem as she is, or at least more anxious about it than he is.

I want to put it a little differently. Neither the husband nor the wife in the first story I related in Chapter 6 are ever going to read this book. They are not going to have to. Whoever initiates the divorce there is not going to be stuck in the sense that they are unable to hold on to the marriage but also unwilling to let go of it. There will be no question in their mind that they want to go forward and end their marriage.

The husband and the wife in the story I related in Chapter 7 are not going to read this book because neither of them is going to be on the horns of the dilemma I posed. This is not to say there will not be problems in their marriage. I told you that she will drive him a little crazy from time to time, as he will her. But their problem is not likely to create a problem in my sense of that term. Neither of them is ever going to consider getting a divorce. Why would they when they are happily married and love one another? Not in the exciting but artificially romantic sense that they did when they got married, but in the best sense of that term.

How can they be happily married if there are problems in their marriage? There are problems in all marriages, just as there are problems in all of our lives. But none of us would say that we do not have a good, worthwhile life because there are problems in it. The same is true when it comes to marriage.

CHAPTER 10

LOVE AT FIRST SIGHT

Love is faster than a speeding bullet.

It would be natural to assume that serious relationships are formed slowly, over time. As the two of them spend more and more time together and get to know one another better, if they each get a lot of positive feedback, the relationship will develop and, if it is a very personal relationship, such as the one under discussion, they will fall in love with one another. In other words, the love that they come to have for one another will be a consequence and a by-product of the development of their relationship.

While it would be natural to assume this, it would be a mistake. To be sure, many couples know each other for a long period of time before they decide to marry, sometimes for many years. But even todays extended wedding announcements in *The New York Times* tell us very little about how the feelings these couples came to have for one another developed. Those announcements only tell us that when those feelings developed much more quickly.

But that is not the point I want to make. What difference does it make whether those feelings, and the decision to marry that the couple make on the basis of them, took place after five years or only five months. In both cases it could be assumed that those feelings and that decision were based on what they had each learned about the other in the period in question. But what if those feelings had developed, and that decision had been made, in five minutes or even five hours? What if it was faster than a speeding bullet? Obviously, that would be a very different matter.

But that is not going to happen, you will say. I would have thought the same thing. At least I would have thought that until I started reading the extended wedding announcements in the Styles Section of *The New York Times*. To be sure, they described instances where those feelings, and the decision that was based on them, developed over an extended period of time. Obviously, that did not surprise me. It suggested that there was a rational basis for those feelings and that decision, as we would have assumed there would be, in this case the knowledge that the parties had acquired about one another over that period of time. What did surprise me was how, time and time again, those feelings, and the decision that was made on the basis of them, developed in literally an instant in time. Since this will be critical to my central argument, namely, that we marry total strangers, I am going to quote from a number of these wedding announcements. If I only quoted from one or two, there is the danger that they might be dismissed as not being representative. That is why I am going to quote from quite a few.

———————

(Both juniors in college, they had enrolled in the same class. As Ms. . . . sat in the classroom with her roommate, she noticed a man saunter in and sit down three rows in front of her.) As her roommate described it, "Vanessa grabbed my arm hard and said, 'I'm going to marry him'." As Vanessa later said, "He looked tough, yet approachable, qualities I've always found attractive."

Needless to say, the fact that the young woman here impulsively said that she was going to marry the young man who sauntered in didn't mean that she actually would. How do I know that she did?

Because I read their wedding announcement in the Styles Section of *The New York Times*.

"Mr. . . . and Ms. . . . found each other at a late-night party in the Hamptons. The mutual attraction was immediate, and in a haze of music and pheromones, they drifted away together to a quiet spot. She touched his shoulder. He held her hand. Then he started talking about mortgages. . . . In a month she was living on his yacht and returned with him to Los Angeles. 'I fell in love pretty much right away', she said. 'He makes me feel like I'm the only one that matters'."

(His comment after they had met at a friend's birthday party.)

"We were spellbound by each other. I couldn't stop thinking how gorgeous she was and how much chemistry we had."

The couple attended a Jewish speed-dating session in which 20 women were seated at different tables. There was an equal number of men, who were allowed to visit each table for three minutes. The first table that Mr. . . . visited was Ms. . . .'s "'There was nothing not to like about her' Mr. . . . said. 'She's smart and she's very beautiful and we instantly had a lot of things in common, like music and a love of theater. It was just an instant connection, one of those indescribable things where there seemed to be lightning striking'."

How long did it take? It took no more than three minutes, because that is all the time they were given.

(A mutual friend introduced him to her and they spoke together for about an hour, after which he took her to a restaurant with some mutual friends of theirs)

"My adrenaline was pumping the minute she sat next to me. Although we were with other friends, she was never more than an arm's length away from me the entire night. It was electric right from the start."

———————

(The two of them were at a bar in Manhattan.)

"'I noticed her from across the room and was suddenly in a haze; it was like everything around me had disappeared', he said. 'I just thought she was beautiful and I was awe struck. I knew I would regret if I didn't go over there and give it a shot.' So he made his move." At the end of the evening, he took her phone number and walked her to the subway. The next day he texted her and they made plans to go out on a first date at a Manhattan restaurant. "'Our conversation was seamless right from the start; we were very comfortable with one another', said Ms. . . ., who shared her first kiss with Mr. . . . that night." "'We've been together ever since'."

———————

(The couple met at a bar in Manhattan. The night was cold and neither of them had much interest in venturing out.)

"But when Mr. . . . spotted Ms. . . . at the bar, he felt the beginning of what he called 'one of those sort of amazing New York evenings'." They began talking and found that they had mutual interests in food and sports, and their outlook on life matched. "'We share a slightly cynical, yet still sort of optimistic, view of the world'," he said. But they had obvious differences, too. "'He is incredibly preppy and I am incredibly not'," she said. "Three hours and forty-two minutes later, when his friends prevailed upon him to move on to another spot, Ms. . . . scribbled out her number for him and then grabbed him by the ears and kissed him. Call me she said'. Fifteen minutes later, he did."

———————

(The couple met at a restaurant in Manhattan.)

"They spoke until the restaurant closed, and decided to continue the conversation at her apartment. 'The next day he took a taxi from my place in Brooklyn back to work in Manhattan' Ms. . . . said. 'I didn't think I would ever hear from him again, but he called me three hours later and asked if I would have dinner with him that night.' Mr. . . ., who lived in Manhattan at the time, returned to Ms. . . .'s home for a second straight night, and never left. 'We loved each other and got each other from the very start,' Ms. . . . said. 'He would start a sentence, and I would finish it. I know that sounds corny, but its true. I was the one who suggested that he stay forever, and we basically began living together.' 'It all happened so fast, but I knew that I had found the missing piece of the puzzle', said Mr. . . . 'She was beautiful and very honest and had a great, straightforward personality' he said. 'When she said something she meant it. Despite the fact that people were telling me to take it slow, I fell in love with her immediately. I knew right away that she was the best thing that ever happened to me'."

———————

(Mr. . . . happened to drop by a friend's home when Ms. . . . was there.)

"'I did a complete thunderbolt thing', Mr. . . . said. 'Our eyes met from across the room,' Ms. . . . said." 'We have been together since that day'."

———————

(The couple met at a wedding reception.)'

"'She had a sense of style I liked', he said of Ms. . . . 'We danced and talked all night.' Ms. . . . then left for an eight-day cruise to the Caribbean. 'We really connected at the reception, and I thought about him on the cruise', she said. 'He was different than all of the other guys I had met in terms of personality. I knew he was the one'."

———————

(The couple met at a conference.)

"'We had an instant rapport,' Ms. . . . remembers. They were also immediately attracted to each other. 'I thought that she was beautiful and charming', Mr. . . . said. For her part, she said she thought he was handsome, and the minute they started talking, she kind of forgot all about the conference. 'Within a few days', Ms. . . . said, 'we were totally inseparable'."

(The couple met at a poetry reading.)

"'It was love at first sight', he said. He waited for a chance to introduce himself and found an opportunity later that night at a bar, where many of the poets had gathered. 'He really didn't talk to anyone else the rest of the night', Ms. . . . recalled. 'He was very funny, and he liked my jokes, and he was very handsome.' After what Ms. . . . described as 'a 20-day, whirlwind courtship,' the couple surprised friends and family by announcing their engagement. 'Our families were shocked,' she said. 'But I told my parents that he was one of the kindest people I had ever met and that we were really in love, and that we were destined to meet'."

(The couple met on a blind date arranged by their parents.)

"Ms. . . . said that she thought that he was 'very handsome' and was surprised at how they hit it off. Drinks and conversation quickly ran into overtime. They closed the restaurant after midnight and headed to what Mr. . . . described as a 'comfortable, divey bar'. The date ended at 4:00 a.m. Before he put her in a cab, Mr. . . . made sure she had a place in her BlackBerry for him the next weekend."

(Mr. . . . lent his home to a law school professor who wanted to have a party for about 100 law students. Mr. . ., who was himself a lawyer, thought that the party might be a good opportunity to meet women.)

"'My bachelor instincts were disappointed', Mr. . . . said, until Helena arrived late that evening'. It was love at first sight, at least for Mr. . . ." Two days after meeting Mr. . ., she received an e-mail from him that began, 'I want to marry you'."

(Ms. . . . was interested in learning more about health care investment banking and asked her brother if he knew anyone she could talk to about it. He arranged for her to meet with Mr. . . .)

"Mr. . . . set up an appointment with Ms. . . ., asking her to meet him at his office before walking to a nearby coffee shop for what both described as an 'information meeting'. But when Ms. . . . did not arrive on time, Mr. . . . became angry. 'Here I was trying to do this girl a favor, and she was late', he said. 'I wasn't happy about it'. But his mood changed the moment Ms. . . . walked through the door and into his life. 'She was so gorgeous, she took my breath away', he said, 'I was completely blown away. It was almost as if I had been struck by a thunder bolt.' They eventually went to the meeting, which lasted five hours."

What is he saying here? (He must be saying something.) What are we to make of this? Obviously, the speaker is not making a statement about the other person. He doesn't know the other person. What he (or she) is expressing is his feeling that the person in question, on his arm, validates and confirms, both to himself and to the world, his image and sense of himself, and thereby completes him, which is why he has allowed that floodgate of feelings to come crashing in. To be sure, he has tried to justify how he feels by telling us that she is "gorgeous" or "beautiful." But that is not necessarily true. It is just his way of validating his feelings. How do I know that his description of her is not accurate? Because I saw a picture of her (or him) in *The New York Times*.

Needless to say, this is not how we expect these feelings to arise. Rather, we assume that the love the two of them develop for one another is a consequence and by-product of what goes on between them, and what they learn about one another, over time. Otherwise it has no basis. And if it is not a rational decision in any sense of that term, it could not possibly be a sound basis for their marriage. No wonder that they may later get divorced.

It could be argued that this is not the whole story. After all, they are not getting married the day they met one another or first had those mutual feelings. In most instances they aren't going to get married for some time. After all, it is commonly necessary to book the hotel or other facility where the wedding will take place many months in advance. In that time, they are going to be spending a great deal of time together and getting to know one another a lot better. They are also going to have an opportunity to see things that they couldn't have seen or known when they first met. If what they learn doesn't please them or, worse, if it is a telltale sign of possible danger ahead, they can change their mind and end their relationship or call off the wedding. There are couples who do that all of the time. They even do that after the wedding invitations have already been sent out. So even if they acted in too much haste and made a mistake, they will have an adequate opportunity to correct it. In other words, the marriages that were ill conceived will be weeded out in time

Unfortunately, there is a problem with this suggestion. If the marriages that were ill conceived will be weeded out, as the argument suggests, what we should be left with are marriages that stand on a firm foundation. What we should be left with are not those marriages which, if they had not been weeded out, would have ended in divorce, but those that will go the distance.

But, as we know, the marriages that we will be left with will not all go the distance. On the contrary, almost half of them will end in divorce. If that is the case, the weeding out process that we were relying on is not a reliable guide when it comes to those marriages that will make it and those that will not. If the chances are only fifty-fifty, we could have done as well by flipping a coin.

The wedding announcements in the Styles Section of *The New York Times* are always accompanied by a picture of the couple. But the pictures that accompany the announcements that I have quoted from are different from those that accompany the traditional announcements. It is not just that they are larger because these announcements take up two columns rather than just one. They are different because they are more animated and alive. In the traditional announcements, the couple are side by side looking out at us. Thus, though they are smiling, with rare exception they are not smiling at one another. In the extended announcements that I have quoted from, the couple is far more engaged with one another, and the picture of them is far more reflective of what the announcement has said about them than were the pictures in the more traditional announcements, which said literally nothing about them other than name, rank and serial number. Put another way, the hope and expectation that they are experiencing, and their romantic love for one another, is written all over their faces. To be sure, there was hope and expectation in the pictures that accompanied the traditional announcements as well. But it was more muted and more formal.

If we were to take a picture of the two of them today, what would it look like? We don't know. Couples don't submit announcements to the Styles Section of *The New York Times* five or ten years after their marriage reporting how they are doing. Nevertheless, every so often—perhaps once a year—the Styles Section will contain an article highlighting a number of couples whose wedding announcements appeared there five or ten years ago, together with a picture of them (and their children, if they have any). It is a far different picture than appeared with their wedding announcement. It is completely devoid of the hope and expectation, and their romantic feelings for one another, that so characterized the earlier picture. It is just a picture of the two of them and their children

I don't want to be misunderstood here. I am not suggesting that couples who have been married for five or ten years (or longer), who would now describe their relationship with one another in more modest and more realistic terms, do not have good, satisfying marriages. On the contrary, I am willing to assume that they do. I am just saying that their relationship today has little if any resemblance to what they envisioned it would be when they first got married. How could it when, in most instances, it was based on little more than a romantic illusion which, because it was just that, could not possibly have lasted for more than a relatively short period of time?

CHAPTER 11

COMMON INTERESTS

We have everything in common. No, you
actually have very little in common.

It is not necessary to pursue the matter further. I think that we would all agree that the couples whose stories I related in the last chapter could not possibly have known enough about one another to make what we would describe as an intelligent decision when it came to whether or not they should move forward and get married. They knew very little, and in some instances nothing, about one another. As we say, they were flying blind.

But in each instance these were intelligent, educated men and women, who were in the habit of making important decisions in their lives based on their sound judgment, not on the basis of mere whim. And this was certainly an important decision in their lives. In fact, if we asked them, they would no doubt say that it was probably the most important decision that they would ever make in their lives.

So how do we explain it? Again, these announcements give us the answer. Obviously, the parties didn't pretend that they knew one another very well when they made that important decision. They acknowledged that they didn't know one another at all. If that is the case, how did they avoid the necessary implication when it comes to this, namely, that there was no rational basis for their decision and that, as I said, it was based on nothing more than whim? What they did is very interesting, and just as revealing. They claimed that, even in that short period of time, they learned that they had a great deal in common, and let that stand substitute for the fact that they didn't and couldn't suggest that they knew one another very well. I'm not talking about the fact that they learned that they were cut from the same cloth, as I previously put it. They would not have thought in those terms. Rather, that they had significant interests in common. Again, let us listen to them.

(Friends introduced them at a restaurant in New York.)
"We just had a great time; we instantly felt comfortable with one another. . . . He's very articulate, kind and sincere. He had a genuine interest in me and my family and friends." Three days later, Mr. . . . called and asked Ms. . . . out, this time just the two of them. "We had so much in common, shared beliefs, shared interests, shared goals," Ms. . . . said. 'I liked how naturally we spoke to each other, which resulted in us closing down restaurants and bars all over town."

———————

(The couple met on Match.com.)
"After a week of exchanging messages, Ms. . . . agreed to a date. They met at a bar in Boston and connected over their shared passions (wanderlust, adventure and public service), and talked for three hours. He walked her to the subway, but she would not let him kiss her. Three days later, after their second date and their first kiss, Ms. . . . said she knew that she was in love. 'It sounds almost storybookish, but it felt like I could finally feel my heart pounding,' she said, 'Normally, you go around life, you don't think about your heart beating, but I could feel it in my chest. It felt like it was growing'."

———————

(They were on a blind date set up by mutual friends at a restaurant in New York.)

"We had a lot in common, and I knew right away that I wanted to go on a second and third date with him,' said Ms. . . ., who learned that night that he, like she, valued family, loved traveling and was a Democrat'."

"It all started with all of our common interests," he said. "But more and more I realized what a sweet soul she was and wanted to spend every possible minute with her."

(They had met at a party and two months later went out on a first date to an art gallery in Washington, D.C.)

"As they roamed the galleries, they discovered that they shared 'a deep respect for our Catholic faith, a love of cooking and entertaining, an appreciation for yoga, a passion for travel and a desire to see the world', Ms. . . . said. 'I fell in love with him that day'."

The couples whose stories I have related were not that careful. They conflated their values and their interests. Thus, in the last announcement, their Catholic faith is a value. Their desire to see the world, on the other hand, is an interest. It makes no difference. In each instance they are citing them as being important in the sense that they demonstrated that there was a sound basis for how they felt and the decision that they made on the basis of that.

But the distinction I have just made is important in another sense. Obviously, the wife in the last wedding announcement that I quoted from (and I will assume her husband as well) would not have considered anyone who did not share her Catholic faith as a suitable candidate. But if she excluded all of those who did not share her

Catholic faith, that would still have left her with an incredibly large number of people to choose from. How does she decide between them? Based on their other common values and interests. (I include values here because, in other instances, the lack of common values might not be a disqualifier. For example, the wife in the previous announcement might have been willing to marry her husband even if he had been a Republican rather than a Democrat.)

But, except where they disqualify someone to be in the running, these common values and interests are not that important. To be sure, having common values and interests will certainly add to a marriage. But they are not the make or break issues in a marriage. In the terms here, though we have been led to believe otherwise, they are not the things that account for those marriages that end in divorce and those that go the distance.

Let me give one example here. Personal hygiene is important to both of them. They both take a shower every morning and brush their teeth after every meal. But brushing their teeth and showering is not what their marriage is all about. To be sure, if their habits here are too different (particularly if one's habits are very distasteful to the other), that might create a problem. But not just because they are different. After all, there are couples who have very happy marriages despite the fact that one of them is a vegetarian and the other is not.

The point is that future husbands and wives put far more significance in these common values and interests than they deserve. They do that because they are reaching for straws. They are trying to justify a decision that has no justification. How could it when they are total strangers?

CHAPTER 12

LOVE

Love is the argument that admits of no argumentation

To be sure, husbands and wives who marry believe they are making a rational decision based on their sound judgment. That is why they have such confidence in their decision. That is why, despite what the statistics suggest, namely, that it is only a gamble, they have every confidence that their marriage will be a happy one and go the distance.

But the decision was not based on their sound judgment. There was literally no judgment involved at all. How could there have been when they married a total stranger who they knew so little about? How could there have been when the two of them had so little in common? How could there have been when their marriage represented the terrible mismatch which they now consider it to be. What, then, accounted for it? The announcements of their marriage in the Styles Section of *The New York Times* said it all. They fell in love.

Though we do not appreciate this as we should, we do not normally view falling in a positive light. How could we? By definition, it means being left in a state where we are helpless and out of control. Who would ever want to be in such a state?

Why do husbands and wives view it other than that? Why do they put this state of helplessness on a pedestal and worship it? In part, I have already answered that in Chapter 5 (What Does It Mean To Say I Love you?). But there is more to the story. We put love on a pedestal and worship it because we have been brought up to do that. To be sure, that was not always the case. On the contrary, until fairly recently, falling in love was considered to be symptomatic of a mental illness. Since the early 18th century, however, we have been led to believe that the love that we feel for someone represents not only the fullest expression of ourselves but also the purest, most noble and very best in ourselves. In short, romantic love is a godly virtue, and to say to someone that you love them is the highest compliment you can pay them.

But there is still more to it than that. As I noted earlier, the love that each of them professes to the other comes with feelings. To be more accurate, it overwhelms them with feelings that render them literally helpless. That is why they refer to what they are experiencing as their having "fallen" in love.

There is another side to this as well. Those feelings that so overwhelm them and make them feel helpless also empower them. As I noted earlier, neither of them has ever felt so full and so at one with themselves in their lives. Moreover, all of this is reinforced by the fact that there is a very powerful sexual dimension to those feelings that further caries them away. And that is why love is the argument that admits of no argumentation.

More important, each of them wants to maintain those intoxicating feelings at that feverish pitch. They don't want anything to disturb or diminish them. As a result, though they are not aware of this, they conduct their relationship on a very narrow playing field in an attempt to suppress what might tend to undermine it. That is why the woman in Chapter 7 was not telling the whole story when she said that she did not want her future husband to know that she had a tendency to be anxious because she wanted him to like her. To be sure, there was some truth to that. But what she really didn't want was anything to take place that would disturb the wonderful thing that they had going for them, namely, the intoxicating feelings that they were each experiencing.

I said that, to protect their relationship, the two of them will conduct it on a very narrow playing field. They will do something else as well, which is to incorporate into it a censor that will tend to deflect and annul anything that might have the effect of piercing or dispelling the necessarily fragile illusion they are experiencing. To be sure, there will often be things that will occur that their censor will not be able to effectively block out. Since, as I said, their relationship is operating on the basis of a necessarily fragile illusion, it is always subject to that possibility. If that is the case, one or both of them may decide to end the relationship.

There is one last thing that has to be added, and it is not particularly flattering. I said earlier that we have been brough up to believe that to say to someone that you love them is the highest compliment that you can pay them. I now have to take that back. You are not paying them any compliment. In fact you are not saying anything about them at all. As I said, what you are really expressing is how they make you feel about yourself, which is more full, more alive and more at one with yourself than you have ever felt in your life. And when they smile at you, and put the spotlight on you, those feelings are only reinforced. That is why you want to possess them and have them as your own. That is why, in your profession of love, you have not really paid them any compliment at all. How could you have when it was all about you.

I don't want to be misunderstood. I am not suggesting that it is not possible to salvage out of this something that is valuable and of real worth. Most couples whose marriage goes the distance do. But it is on a different basis. To begin with, as overwhelming as those feelings may be, they are relatively short lived. It has been suggested that they are sustained by certain natural stimulants, principally dopamine, that are sent to the brain. However, these stimulants have a relatively short shelf life. Secondly, given time, husbands and wives get to know one another better and, more important, see one another more accurately. And when they do, what they see is not an illusory abstraction, but a real flesh and blood person, warts and all.

Sometimes they do not like what they see. Even though they did not see it at the time, they now realize that they were not only total strangers when they married but also mismatched. More to the point, sometimes they cannot live with what they see, which is why they will move forward and end their marriage by getting a divorce.

But there are others who, if they are lucky, will be able to fashion what they have been left with into something of value. As I will argue at a later point, one of the pre-conditions for this will be their belief that, warts and all, they are married to someone who they basically like, someone who, despite the fact that they can drive them a little crazy from time to time, is basically a decent person. Secondly, they will have something that they didn't have when they got married, which is a shared life and history together. And that history will include the fact that they had someone who was there for them, and who cared for them, that entire time. This too will help to leave them with something of value, regardless of how the relationship was initially formed.

CHAPTER 13

SUCCESSIVE MARRAIGES

We do not have one marriage. We have successive marriages.

Since we only marry our husband or wife once, it is natural for us to assume that the two of us have only one marriage. However, as I will argue, we have more than one marriage. We have what I will refer to as successive marriages. Moreover, these successive marriages are not the same. In the terms here, they pose different problems for us.

To be sure, as a general rule husbands and wives are not aware that they have successive marriages. That is because these successive marriages appear seamless. As a result, they do not realize that they have left one marriage and gone into another. But they have. Thus, a couple's marriage after their first child is born is different than it was, in the early years of their marriage, before they had children. Again, their marriage after the wife returns to work, whether on a part time or full time basis, is different than it was when she was a stay-at-home mother. Their marriage after their children are older and more independent is different than it was when they were younger. It is different again when all of their children have completed their education and gone out to work, even if one or more of them continue to live at home. It is different still when their children marry, particularly when they begin to have children of their own. And it is also different once the two of them retire from work and enter the last phase of their life together. Issues of health aside, many married couples will say that this is the best time of their lives.

There are times when they are more aware of the change that has taken place in their lives, even though they do not think of it in the terms that I have put it, namely, as successive marriages. That is when the new phase of their marriage creates problems that did not exist in the previous phase.

As I indicated earlier, many couples will talk about children, and how important they are to them, before they get married. But they will talk more in terms of abstractions. The problem, as I noted previously, is that those abstractions will not tell them who will change their diapers., take them to school, or do their homework with them. Nor will they tell them how they will each react to the problems that their children can represent. (Abstractions are abstract.) How can they know that when they do not have any children? Be that as it may, their different adaptive styles (and as I will later refer to them, their different emotional dispositions) and how they each relate to problems that their children may have or represent, can become a problem for the two of them.

I will give three examples of this. There are parents who will have all of the patience in the world when it comes to their children. But there are also parents who will not. On the contrary, there will be parents who will become frustrated and just as annoyed when their two year old son or daughter acts like a two year old boy or girl.. They just don't have the patience that their husband or wife has. If that is the case, the other parent (we will call her the wife) in order to accommodate the situation, may take over the parenting responsibilities. Unfortunately, while that may solve one problem, it may only create another. The wife may now become resentful that her husband's withdrawal, which she at least has in part facilitated, has left her with more of the parenting responsibilities than she previously had, which were more than his to begin with. That is going to add a burden to their relationship that didn't exist in the previous phase of their marriage.

The next examples are a little different but can create an even bigger problem. When husbands and wives have the same basic attitudes toward their children, that will tend to strengthen the bonds between them. But the opposite can be the case when they don't view them in the same way, particularly if one of them resents the fact that the other displays little interest in, and gives little time and attention to, their children.

Their different approaches to their children can also become an issue if they respond to a problem concerning their children in different ways. I will give two examples of this. Not uncommonly, infants can cry through the night. That will not be a problem if they both react to their child's crying in the same way. But it will become a problem if the wife's reaction will be to go in and comfort the child and the husband's reaction will be to leave the child alone and let him cry himself to sleep, particularly if he objects to the wife going into the child's room to comfort him. For her part, she will become equally upset if she does not go into the room and comfort him. Nor will they ever be able to resolve this difference between them, and since it involves their child, who they both have strong feelings about, this is going to create a problem for the two of them.

This can come up in another way as well. Children sometime run into difficulties. It can be a disciplinary problem in school. It can be an illness that a child develops. That in and of itself is not the problem. The problem is that a husband and wife can react very differently when faced with one of these difficulties, particularly when it is not clear what the cause of it is. If that is the case, it can cause each of them to fall back upon, and to propose, diametrically opposite solutions to the problem, the husband going into a state of denial and defending his child against the school and the wife accepting the school's claim that it is their child who created the problem.

Why have I used these as examples of what can take place that will cause problems to arise in a marriage? Because it would never have occurred to them that they would. After all, one of the things that they had in common, and that they looked to as assurance that their marriage would be a strong one, was the fact that having children was so important to both of them.

But I used them for two other reasons as well. The first was to underscore my suggestion that we have successive marriages. The second, and more important reason was to underscore the fact that all marriages (relationships) take place in a state of balanced-imbalance. There are considerations that are holding the two of them together and considerations that have the tendency to pull them apart.

To be sure, if we are in a basically sound marriage, we may not even be aware of these undermining considerations. In a basically sound marriage they will appear as nothing more than minor annoyances. If they are more than minor annoyances, if the marriage is basically a happy one, the two of them may be able to deal with the problems that the new phase of their marriage has brought with it. In an unhappy marriage, however, one of them will be painfully aware of them. That is why they are so desperately unhappy.

The point is that these competing considerations do not play themselves out in the same way in our successive marriages, What was not a problem at one stage can become a problem in another. That is what I was referring to when I said earlier that the appropriate question was not why they were getting divorced but why they were getting divorced now rather than two years ago, when the wife first brought up the idea in her mind, or two years from now when their youngest child will go off to college. After all, the considerations that had the possibility of undermining their marriage were there throughout their successive marriages. As I put it, the seeds that would take root and undermine their marriage had in most instances been planted before they got married. Thus, it was not a question of whether there was a possibility that they would end their marriage. There was always that possibility. The question was if and when those considerations that had the possibility of undermining their marriage would get the upper hand.

This was dramatically brought home to me with a couple whose divorce I mediated. The wife was 21 and the husband 22 when they married. It was now 36 years later and their four children, who they had in rapid succession following their marriage, were now all grown and on their own. Although the wife had been a stay at home mother for many years when her children were young, she was now employed and had been for some time.

This should have been a relatively easy matter. Since their children were now adults, there was no issue of custody or child support. Though the husband earned more than his wife, the disparity in their incomes was not such that the husband was going to be required to make a payment to the wife for her support and maintenance, and she didn't expect any. Thus, the only issues were the division of their assets, which consisted of their home, which was going to be sold, the division of their other assets, which consisted principally of the husband's future pension and other retirement benefits (the wife had acquired none from her employment), and the satisfaction of their debts, which were quite considerable and which were going to be paid for from the proceeds from the sale of their home. As I said, this should have been a relatively easy matter.

However, nothing was easy when it came to the husband here. As he had been his own worst enemy in his marriage so, too, he was his own worst enemy in his divorce. He was a classic example of a branch that breaks when it cannot bend. Thus, though the last thing he wanted was to get divorced, there wasn't anything that he had been prepared to do to prevent it. Worse, he made getting it many times more difficult than it had to be. For her part, the wife, who had always conducted herself in a dignified manner, was willing to make accommodations and compromises with life in order to get it done. The husband, however, would make none. On the contrary, he kept throwing roadblocks in the way at every turn.

Throughout the mediation, and although I knew better, I kept asking myself why and how the wife had stayed in the marriage as long as she had. Her husband didn't seem to have a redeeming quality, and it was hard to see what satisfaction the wife could have gotten out of the marriage. To add to it, although my experience had been that, despite the difference in their formal levels of education, most husbands and wives were of fairly equal intelligence, the wife here was heads and shoulders above her husband in that regard. She was also far more dignified.

When we finally got done, and the two of them had signed their separation agreement and all of the other papers in connection with their divorce, the husband got up and quickly left the room while the wife was collecting her papers. After she had done so, she turned to me and said, "He changed so much."

What did that mean and for whose benefit was the wife telling me that? She certainly didn't owe me an explanation. And she had to know that not only was I not judgmental, but also that I held her in high regard. While her husband may have been a very poor excuse for a human being, she was a very fine person. That is what made their marriage so hard to explain.

But, as I quickly realized, she was not saying this for my benefit. She was saying this for her own. Each of us goes through our lives telling stories to ourselves about ourselves. It is our way of making sense of our lives and it is very important that we keep our stories straight. That is what she was trying to do. That is what every divorcing husband and wife has to do. She had to come to terms with the fact that she had stayed married to a man who was a very poor excuse for a human being for as long as she had. What she was telling me (really telling herself) was that he had not always been like this. He had changed.

He hadn't changed. He had always been the same very poor excuse for a human being that he was today. In my terms, the wife here who, for various reasons, had been unwilling to allow the considerations that were undermining her marriage in the previous stages of their marriage to get the upper hand, was now willing to allow them to do so. Since it would have been too difficult if not impossible for her to explain it in the terms that I did, she explained it in her own terms. It didn't make any difference that her explanation didn't bear any resemblance to reality. If that is what she had to do in order to keep her story straight, who cared and what difference did it make?

I

Up until this point, I have talked about competing considerations that play themselves out over the course of a marriage. But there are also considerations of a different kind that will also have an effect on the relationship during what I have described as the successive marriages that a couple will live through. These are not things that the parties could have known about if they had paid closer attention. These are things that they couldn't have known about unless and until the situation arose.

Let me give an example of this. Their youngest child has just gone off to college. If the husband has worked throughout the marriage, this will not necessarily pose a problem for them. He will continue to do what he has always done. But if the wife has been a full time homemaker, she will no longer be able to do that. They just did away with her job, and this may pose a problem for her. What is she going to do with her time now that she is no longer a homemaker in the sense that she was before their youngest child went off to college? Whatever she is going to do, her options are not going to be what they were twenty years earlier. Rather, as most women in her position quickly find, they will be far more limited. From a practical standpoint, they may even be non-existent.

Again, this is not something that they thought about, or could have thought about, before they got married and had children. Rather, they just went about the business of their lives and made such decisions and accommodations as the circumstances required. But the wife will have to deal with it now. And if the wife will have to do that, her husband may have to do that as well.

The point is that the problems that a husband and wife will encounter in what I have described as their successive marriages can play out differently over time. That is because, in my terms, in a certain sense each of their successive marriages is a different marriage.

I don't want to be misunderstood here. I am not suggesting that the fact that they have successive marriages will lead to their divorce.

I am only pointing to it to underscore the tremendous difference between the romantic illusion that characterized their relationship before they married and the reality of their relationship after they have passed through that romantic illusion. You would see it if the Styles Section of The New York Times had a picture of the two of them today and you compared it with the picture of the two of them that accompanied their wedding announcement ten years ago. They would not have that same excited look on their faces now that they had then. They would not even be looking at one another. They would just be two people looking out at you.

CHAPTER 14

MARRYING AN ALIEN FROM ANOTHER PLANET

Husbands and wives are constitutionally different

As I have argued, though the powerful feelings that overwhelm men and women who are in love causes them to believe that they are as one, since they are different people and therefore have their differences, that is just an illusion. Until now, to make this point I have characterized the two of them as being mismatched. I am now going to go further. I am going to argue that husbands and wives are constitutionally different or, as I will put it, that they have significantly different emotional dispositions and adaptive styles, so much so that it is as if they were each marrying an alien from another planet.

I appreciate the fact that this suggestion is not going to be taken kindly. On the contrary, it will be summarily dismissed as being insulting and offensive. After all, the so called "differences" between men and women, and between whites, blacks and other groups, has been disgracefully invoked throughout history to justify the subordinate treatment that has been accorded to them. When it came to blacks, it was even used to justify their enslavement. So I want to make it clear that I am not talking about any characteristic, such as intelligence, which could possibly be used to justify this. In other words I am not talking about differences in terms of better or worse. I am just talking about differences. Moreover, we acknowledge those differences all of the time without taking offense. Thus, if I am correct, the average height, weight and strength of a woman is less than that of a man, which is why women's basketball teams play other women's basketball teams rather than men's basketball teams. And the same is true of most athletic competitions. Nor do any of us have a problem with that. On the contrary, we agree that it is appropriate. Moreover, the fact that we may object to female athletes being paid less than male athletes doesn't cause us to object to their playing against other women. So it is in that sense, and only that sense, that I am pointing out the differences between men and women.

This brings me to what will be the second objection to my suggestion. Even if there are the emotional and other differences that I claim there are in marriages between men and women, it will be argued that the same cannot be true in a same sex marriage. I acknowledge that, on the face of it, that objection has to seem correct. Nevertheless, I am going to argue that, ironically, the same is true when it comes to same sex marriages as well. However, since I appreciate that the argument I am going to introduce will understandably go against the grain, I am going to start by talking about marriages between a man and a woman.

If I were to suggest that, as a general rule, even though the situation has changed somewhat in the last half century, women spend significantly more time than men in caring for the couple's children, even when they are employed on a full time basis outside the home, while we might object to this arrangement, we would not take issue with my suggestion that it is true, any more than we would take exception to the suggestion that men spend more time maintaining the home (I said maintaining, not cleaning) than women do. This is not to say that men do not cook meals for their children or clean up after them, any more than it is to say that some women do not mow the lawn. It is just to say that their respective contributions can be different just as they can be more or less. Nor am I saying that these differences will or will not be a problem, though I will say that it is very unlikely that they will lead to their divorce. It is what I have referred to as their different emotional dispositions and adaptive styles that will. It is that one of them is a woman and the other is a man, and the fact that men and women are different. It is also due to the fact that, as a general rule, the differences that I am talking about tend not to manifest themselves before the two of them marry or, if they do, for the reasons that I have given, that they manifest themselves far less.

I am purposely going to start with what will seem a strange example. I am talking about sex, and I bring it up because, as marriage counselors will tell you, it is a complaint that they run into time and time again in their dealings with husbands and wives. But I bring it up for another reason. It is because it is not a complaint that either of the parties will bring up before they marry. Before they marry neither of them can get it quickly enough or often enough. However, it is very different after they marry. As their marriage counselor will testify, the frequency of their sexual relations is now very often a problem, she complaining that he almost always wants it, he complaining that she almost never does.

What does this have to do with what I argue is their different emotional dispositions? It supports my suggestion, first, that men and women are different in significant ways, second, that those differences are not as apparent (as significant) prior to their marriage as they become after their marriage and, third, that those differences contribute to the problems they are now having in their marriage.

What accounts for these differences. If we were talking about the fact that the average weight and height of men and women are different we would not ask why. They are just different, and it has nothing to do with their emotional dispositions. But their respective attitudes toward sex is different, particularly given the fact that while their attitude was very much the same before they married, as marriage counselors who work with husbands and wives will tell you, they are commonly very different after they marry. We could say that the reason for this is that, for men, sex is a means of establishing something (a man's superior position) whereas, for women sex is a means of securing something (the protection that having a man provides).

Does it have anything to do with the fact that a man is generally on top and a woman on the bottom or the fact that a man enters a woman rather than that a woman enters a man? Is there something else that explains it? Who knows? But we would be very uncomfortable with any of those suggestions. Our romantic view of marriage and the fact that we are part of the animal kingdom, where two males engage in mortal battle with one another to determine who will have the right to enter the waiting female, are not very compatible. As a result, we are very uncomfortable with the question of whether men and women have different attitudes towards sex and, if so, why, even though their different attitudes toward sex so often becomes a problem in their marriage.

But there are other differences between men and women as well. They have different interests. For example, as a general rule, watching the super bowl (and other sporting events) is much more important to men than it is to women. Does that mean that they don't both attend the same super bowl party? No, they commonly do. But there are two aspects to that event, the super bowl and the super bowl party, and the game (the male contest) is generally more important to men and the party (the social event) to women.

And I could go on and on. Both men and women have friends. But men do not generally spending endless amounts of time on the phone with their friends. Women do. The same is true of clothes. Men buy clothes for themselves just as women do. But they do not generally make a career of it as many women do.

This brings me to same sex marriages. I appreciate the fact that, on the face of it, the fact of same sex marriage would seem to undercut my argument that men and women are different—in the terms that I have put it, have different emotional dispositions—and that these differences (in my terms, the differences that they bring to the marriage) later become a problem.

To be sure, that would be the case if men's and women's emotional dispositions were drawn from different pools, a white one when it comes to women and a black one when it comes to men. But that is not the case and I am not suggesting that. They are drawn from the same source, but that source is better represented as being a very long, narrow channel filled with a substance that starts out on the left as white and then, when it proceeds to the right, becomes light grey, then medium grey, then grey, then light black, then medium black, and finally, completely black.

Men and women can both be constituted from the substance along any portion of the channel. In other words, it is not completely either/or. Nevertheless, in the case of women, they are more likely to be constituted from that portion of the substance principally on the left and, for men, from that portion of the substance principally on the right, which accounts for their different emotional dispositions.

But those different emotional dispositions are not limited to opposite sex marriages. As I said, it is not either/or. They can characterize same sex marriages as well. In a marriage between two women, they can both be from that portion of the substance principally on the left, but in one case much further toward the left and in the other much further toward the center. And the same is true in a marriage between two men, except in the opposite direction. In fact, when you meet a same sex couple, it is usually quite apparent who is the "wife" in the relationship (who has more of the emotional disposition of a woman) and who is the "husband" in the relationship (who has more of the emotional disposition of a man).

But what of a transexual who undergoes surgery to change his or her gender. Doesn't that contradict my suggestion? Absolutely not. On the contrary, it supports it.

A transexual is a person who believes that he or she was born with the wrong body. They are really a woman but they were born with the body of a man. That is why they are undergoing surgery.

They are not really a woman. Their body is a testament to that. It is just that, in the terms that I have put it, their emotional disposition was drawn principally from the left side of the stream rather than from the right side of the stream.

It is not necessary to belabor the point. Though the romantic haze which so characterizes their relationship persuades them that they are both cut from the same cloth, they are not. No two people are. But if, on top of their other differences, they have what I characterized as different emotional dispositions, that only complicates the situation even more. Since it is literally impossible for someone to change his or her emotional disposition, it is very difficult to effect a compromise between them. That is why the mental health professionals they turn to for help are so often of little or no help. But I am getting ahead of myself.

CHAPTER 15

PARRALEL LIVES

As we were separate people before we got married,
so too we will be separate people after we get married

Husbands and wives invariably feel as if they are one when they get married. It is as if there was no clear line that divided them. Plato famously described that in the Symposium. Originally, men and women had been joined together as one. However, because of a transgression on their part, Zeus divided each of them into two. It was then their fate to wonder throughout the world in search of their other half—their "soul mate"—until they found and were united with them.

Men and women who marry commonly refer to their future husband and wife in those terms. As one husband put it in their wedding announcement, it was as if there was no boundary between them and they were going to lead one life together rather than two.

This is another illusion that husbands and wives buy into. As they were separate and different people before they got married, so too they will be separate and different people after they get married, except that they will now lead two separate, parallel lives that will come together and then move apart over the course of their marriage. To be sure, they will get to know one another very well after they marry, so much so that they will know how the other will react, and what he or she will say and do. But in an important sense, their husband or wife will be a very different person than the one they thought they knew when they married. Moreover, it will never be possible to know their husband or wife completely. They will each always be somewhat of a stranger to the other. That is because they can only view their husband or wife from the outside and not, as they view themselves, from the inside. That is because each of them has a private life. That is why the two of them will always lead separate, parallel lives rather than one.

This is not a problem. It certainly will not lead to their divorce. On the contrary, it is a necessary condition to their maintaining their marriage. As they go in different directions when they leave for work in the morning to pursue their separate careers, so too will they go in different directions when they pursue their separate interests, she perhaps to attend her book club or to go to a PTA meeting, he to go to a sporting event or to play cards with some of his friends. When they are through, they will come back together again to have dinner, to watch television, to read a book, or to be intimate with one another.

You can see this difference when they go out to dinner at a restaurant. You always know whether the couple at the next table is married or not. Not because they are in one another's laps if they are not married. But because of the constant interaction between them and because of the state of animation that characterizes that interaction. As I said, it is almost as if the two of them were one.

The same will not be true if the couple is married to one another. There will not be the constant interaction or state of animation. Rather, you will just see two people having dinner together. This is no reflection on the state of their relationship. It will be true of the most happily married couples. This will become apparent if the couple at the next table is waiting for friends to join them. Before they arrive they will conduct themselves as if they were going to have dinner alone. However, the minute their friends arrive, the four of them will immediately become engaged in animated conversation.

The parallel lives that very unhappily married husbands and wives lead are different. In some instances they are like railroad tracks that proceed in the same direction but never touch. This was dramatically brought home to me when my wife and I were having dinner in a restaurant one night. There was a couple sitting at a table across from us. Since they seemed to be close to our age, I assumed that, like us, they had been married for a long time. Though they sat there together for at least an hour, they never once made eye contact; nor did they ever say a word to one another. They just sat there in absolute silence. That might have been understandable while they were having their dinner. But before their dinner they each had a drink from which they took only occasional sips. Yet there was still not a word spoken between them. It was as if they were total strangers sitting next to one another on a train. If this was how they conducted themselves in public, I could only imagine how they conducted themselves at home.

To be sure, this was an extreme case, and I am not suggesting that many husbands and wives lead their lives in this manner. Nevertheless, there are many couples whose parallel lives never really come together in any meaningful sense, particularly when their children have grown up and moved away, and are more like railroad tracks that proceed in the same direction but never touch. You might say that this is how they solved the problem they were having interacting in their marriage. They just stopped interacting.

CHAPTER 16

ROMANTIC MARRIAGE

If we marry for the reasons we do,
we will divorce for the reasons we do.

There is one other last element that must be added if we are to understand the problem that husbands and wives today face in their marriage. Unlike the factors that I have already enumerated, this is not something that the two of them brought to their marriage. Rather, it is something that they inherited. That is the fact that marriages today, unlike marriages even in the not too distant past, are founded on a very different basis.

Up until this point, I have not addressed this except indirectly. In other words, up until this point I have not addressed how we got from there to here. Rather, I have just presented a picture of marriage today. But it is not possible to understand marriage today unless we have an understanding of marriage in the past. In this and the next chapter I will take a short excursus to explain that.

It is customary to assume that marriage has been a constant throughout history, which is why we have so much difficulty understanding the tremendous changes that took place in the second half of the 20th century when the divorce rate in the United States more than doubled between the early 1960's and early 1980's, and married families were not only made up of men and women, but also of two men or two women, as well as those who lived as a family but did not get married.

Rather than being a static institution, marriage and the family has always been in a state of structural and conceptual change. It is just that, until recently, that change has taken place at such a snail's pace that we barely noticed it. In the context here, the romantic marriage that we so take for granted today was only of recent origin, and it will not be possible for us to understand what has come to be viewed as the crisis in marriage today unless we factor its advent into the equation.

What we are talking about, of course, is the advent of romantic love as the basis for marriage. That being the case, it would be appropriate to indicate its essential characteristics, which were outlined by one student of the family (Lawrence Stone) as follows:

> "The key elements of the romantic love complex are the following: the notion that there is only one person in the world with whom one can fully unite at all levels; the personality of that person is so idealized that the normal faults and follies of human nature disappear from view; love is often like a thunderbolt that strikes at first sight; love is the most important thing in the world, to which all other considerations, particularly material ones, should be sacrificed; and, lastly, the giving of full reign to personal emotions is admirable, no matter how exaggerated and absurd the resulting conduct may appear to others."

Needless to say, romantic love was not the basis of marriage since time immemorial. Rather, it is of very recent origin, representing the working out of large historical and cultural forces that exerted their influence over roughly the last 300 to 350 years, and we are not going to understand what we are witnessing today unless we take them into account.

To be sure, there are local variations in their effect. For example, the rate of divorce in Western Europe is lower than it is in the United States, just as religious affiliation in the United States is greater than it is in Western Europe. But the rate of divorce has risen in both Western Europe and the United States starting in the mid 20th century, just as religious affiliation has declined in both of those places in that same period of time. That is why it is more important to look at those larger historical and cultural forces rather than the local variations if we are to understand what we are now witnessing. That is why it is necessary for me to take a short excursus and go back in time to before these historical and cultural forcers came into play to show how the changes that we are experiencing today came about.

We are talking about marriage and the family in the 13th and 14th centuries. At that time there was no such thing as a nation, or a central government with an army, in the sense that we know it today. There was not even an established police force to keep order. Thus, in the time we are talking about a crime was not, as we would call it today, a crime against society. It was a crime against the family, and justice was effectuated by "revenge," which was carried out by members of the aggrieved person's extended family. As one student of the family (again Lawrence Stone) put it:

> "This was a society where neither individual autonomy or privacy were respected as desirable ideals. It was generally agreed that the interests of the group, whether that of the kin, the village, or later the state, took priority over the wishes of the individual and the achievement of his particular ends . . . Individual freedom of choice ought at all times and in all respects be subordinated to the interests of others, whether lineage, parents, neighbors, kin, Church or state."

Thus, unlike today, men and women didn't marry for love. Getting married was the most important career decision they would make, and it couldn't be left to anything as irrational and transitory as love. As that same student of the family said:

> "As for life itself, it was cheap, and death came easily and often. The expectation of life was so low that it was highly impudent to become too emotionally dependent upon any other human being. Outside court circles, where it flourished, romantic love was in any case regarded by moralists and theologians as a kind of mental illness, fortunately of short duration."

Freud perhaps put it best. As he said, "Isn't what we mean by 'falling in love' a kind of sickness and craziness, an illusion, a blindness to what the loved person is really like?"

We are talking about an agrarian society where the vast majority of the population lived in rural areas, principally on farms, and the basic economic unit was the family consisting of a husband and wife and their children. While each had different roles, they were all essential parts of the basic economic unit, which was to run the farm. As one student of the family (Stephanie Coontz) put it:

> No individual, male or female, could run a farm single-handedly . . . . In addition to plowing, (the husband) spread manure, dug peat for fuel, and harvested crops by hand, swinging heavy sickles or scythes. He threshed the grain, turned the hay and sometimes hired himself out to work the fields of larger landholders. His wife milked the cows, made butter and cheese, fed the chickens and ducks, cleaned and carted wool, prepared flax (a process that involved fifteen steps), brewed beer and carried water. Women also took surplus produce to market, washed their clothing in the village stream and had their grain pounded at the mill. Both men and women helped with the harvest, gleaned the fields, and collected

firewood. Women, like men, hired themselves out as agricultural laborers."

Thus, a husband and a wife were an economic team, and it was each of their ability to contribute to that undertaking, rather than considerations of personal affection, that dictated who he would take as a wife. This was even true in urban areas, though the economic unit functioned somewhat differently. There the economic unit was the shop, small retail business or tavern run by the family, which was generally conducted on the ground floor, the family living (and, in the case of the wife, also working) on the floor or floors above. Moreover, this had been true since time immemorial, which was why there was so little change in the family in the period which we refer to as the middle ages.

But, particularly in rural areas, there were other people involved besides the couple and their immediate family. Mutual aid was a very important part of an agrarian society. Thus, the choice of one's marriage partner had great economic consequences for other members of the community, too great to be left entirely to the couple themselves. As one student of the family (again Stephanie Coontz) put it:

> "Neighbors had many ways to prevent or punish matches they considered inappropriate. The threat of disapproval or ostracism was no small matter when you shared your planting with your neighbors, did your wash together, and used your neighbor's oven to bake your bread. Villagers might even engage in ritual harassment of the offending young couple."

This, of course, was going to change. In time, the decision was going to be left entirely to the young couple themselves, with the former actors in the drama having little knowledge of the decision until after it had been made. This, in turn, was going to lead to the dramatic changes that took place in marriage and family life in the second half of the 20th century.

To understand this, it is necessary to take into account three historic and cultural occurrences that had a profound effect on marriage and family organization in that time. The first was the Industrial Revolution. The second was the Enlightenment. The third was the introduction of the idea of romantic (or companionate) marriage. While it is not hard to understand how the third would have a profound effect on marriage and family life, it is harder to understand how the first and second would. Nevertheless, their influence was tremendous.

The Industrial Revolution changed marriage and family organization from what it had apparently been since time immemorial in two ways. The first was to move the workplace out of the home and into the factory. The second was to cause those who worked in those factories to relocate from small rural areas to large urban areas, often far removed from where they were born and grew up.

But for our purpose (that purpose being to indicate the tremendous changes that took place in marriage and family organization since the beginning of the 19th century that have brought us to where we are today) the industrial revolution had an even more profound effect on the family. It led to the emancipation of children from the control of their families—not just their parents but all of the family members who had previously had an influence over them. This loosening of family influence had started earlier as children were increasingly sent to work as servants or apprentices in the homes of others after a certain age, As one student of the family (again Stephanie Coontz) put it:

> ". . . the spread of wage labor made young people
> less dependent upon their parents for a start in life. A
> man didn't have to delay marriage until he inherited
> land or took over a business from his father. A woman
> could more readily earn her dowry. As day labor
> replaced apprenticeship and provided alternatives

to domestic service, young workers were no longer required to live in a master's home for several years. They could marry as soon as they were able to earn sufficient wages."

By the same token, if young people were less dependent upon their parents for a start in life, they were also less subject to the influence of their parents in terms of whom they married, which was the precondition for marriage based on individual choice.

The second change was the Enlightenment. I said earlier that the expectation of life in the Middle Ages was low. One could not look to this world for it. It could only be anticipated in the next one. Privacy, like individual autonomy, was not expected. How could it be when the average person lived in a one or two room house, where livestock animals were commonly at one end of the room, and bedrooms and even beds were shared. As one student of the family (again Lawrence Stone) in speaking of the home as late as the early sixteenth century, put it:

> "Lacking firm boundaries, it was open to support, advice, investigation and interference from outside, from neighbors and kin; and internal privacy was non-existent. Inside the home the members of the nuclear family were subordinated to the will of its head, and were not closely bonded to each other by warm affective ties. They might feel closer to other members of the kin, to fellow members of a guild, or to friends and neighbors of the same sex whom they met daily in an ale house. It is important to realize that the total amount of affective feeling was limited."

What was true of peasant households was also true of middle class households, which often included servants and lodgers. As another student of the family (again Stephanie Coontz) put it:

> "Few couples could carve out a private space where
> they might take their meals or even conduct their sex
> lives, discreet from other household members."

Moreover, what was true today, was true yesterday and what was true today would be true tomorrow. Everything always stayed the same.

As I said, the advent of the Enlightenment changed all that. In its simplest terms, the Enlightenment had five very significant effects. First, it changed the world into a secular one. Second, it elevated the importance of individual life. Third, it placed an emphasis on privacy. Fourth, it introduced the concept of equality. Finally it led to the idea of progress.

The focus changed from the next life to this one, which is what I mean when I say that it changed the outlook to a more secular one. As Isaac Newton taught us, the world was not to be understood or explained on the basis of divine guidance or intervention, but on the basis of natural law, in this case on the basis of gravity and motion.

The importance of individual life was also steadily elevated. As John Locke taught us, we were not required to live under the rule of a repressive despot. Rather, we had the right to life, liberty and property, which was translated into the United States Declaration of Independence as life, liberty and the pursuit of happiness.

That in turn gave rise to the increased emphasis on privacy. (In the early 18th century, starting in England, it gave rise to the "calling card." At least amongst the rich and royalty, rather than just showing up unannounced at someone's home, as had been the custom until that time, the person desiring to visit, or more commonly his servant, would deliver their calling cared to a servant of the house in question and then return to their home and wait for an invitation.)

It also led to an emphasis on equality which had never before been thought of or accepted as one of our core values. To be sure, it would take a long time to establish equality between the sexes. This was still a patriarchal society. But the seeds had been planted. Finally, the concept of "progress" was created. Tomorrow was not going to be like today. It was going to be better.

But it was the third historical occurrence, which was an outgrowth of the first two, that was the most significant. That was the introduction of the idea of romantic marriage, also referred to as companionate marriage, which took place in the 18th century and early 19th century in Western Europe and the United States. As one student of the family (again Stephanie Coontz) put it:

> "By the end of the 1700's personal choice of partners had replaced arranged marriages as a social ideal, and individuals were encouraged to marry for love. For the first time in five thousand years marriage came to be seen as a private relationship between two individuals rather than one link in a larger system of political and economic alliances. The measure of a successful marriage was no longer how big a financial settlement was involved, how many useful in-laws were acquired, or how many children were produced, but how well the family met the needs of its individual members. Where once marriage had been seen as the fundamental unit of work and politics, it was now viewed as a refuge from work, politics and community obligations."

At the center of this dramatic change was what one student of the family (Robert N, Polhemus) referred to as "erotic faith", "an emotional conviction, ultimately religious in nature, that meaning, value, hope and even transcendence can be found through love— erotically focused love, the kind we mean when we say that people are in love." As he said:

> "Because doubt about the value of life had been a human constant, historically people have always needed some kind of faith. And with the spread of

secularism since the eighteenth century, erotic faith,
as diverse and informal as it may be, has given to some
a center and sometimes a solace that were traditionally
offered by organized religion and God."

There are three other important changes that took place in the period in question that must be taken into account. The first was a dramatically different attitude toward children. Though it will be difficult for us today to understand this, children were considered to be inherently sinful. The belief in the innate depravity of children was so strong that parents were instructed that it was their duty to break their children's will and thereby repress their innate impulse to sin. This was not only effectuated by strict discipline but by corporal punishment as well, and gave rise to a guiding principle when it came to child rearing, namely, "Spare the rod and spoil the child," and the practice of repeated flogging that became the standard practice in English public schools, even for minor offenses. In fact, well into the 20th century, conduct which today would be considered child abuse and constitute an indictable offense was accepted as nothing more than routine.

Second, children in the time that I am talking about were not considered to be children in our sense of that term. They were just little adults. And it was not too long (generally by the age of seven) before they would begin to perform some of the chores that their mothers and fathers performed, or, as later occurred, usually between the ages of 10 and 14, were sent off to work as servants or apprentices in other people's homes. In other words, there was no such thing as that long period of time, which we refer to today as a child's adolescence, in which a child was sheltered from the adult world. That too was going to change.

Third, a wife's role was not restricted to being a parent to her children as it increasingly became after the advent of the industrial revolution and the move from a rural society to a more urban one. As I said, in the time I am referring to her role as mother to her children was only one of her many roles and the others were even more essential to the well-being of the basic family unit, As time went on, however, her role as mother to her children would become more central.

Finally, as her role as mother to her children became more central, and as she invested more of herself in it, she would also become more central in their lives. More importantly, they would also become more central in the life of the family. Students of the family are not of one mind when it comes to the affection that parents had for their children in the Middle Ages, when it has estimated that fifteen to twenty percent of infants died in the first year of life, approximately one-third died before attaining the age of five years, and as many as fifty percent died before they were ten years of age. Regardless, starting as early as the 16th century, there is evidence of a significant increase in the affection of parents toward their children, By the 19th century the child centered home had become well established. Today husbands and wives will tell you that their children are the most important thing in their lives, as is evidenced by both the emotional and financial investment that they make in them. Thus, children were not just another mouth to feed or another pair of hands to help. They were a godsend.

The other important change in the family, which followed from the ones which I have enumerated, was the creation of what became known as husbands' and wives' "separate spheres" and the "cult of female purity." As one student of the family (again Stephanie Coontz) put it:

> "As the division of a husband's wage-earning activities and a wife's household activities grew, so too did the sense that men and women lived in different spheres, with man's sphere divorced from domesticity and a woman's from the 'economy' . . . Many men and women came to believe that wives should stay at home . . . because home was a sanctuary in which women could be sheltered from the turmoil of economic and political life. Conversely, the domestic

sphere became a place where husbands could escape the materialistic preoccupations of the workday world."

This, of course, was the model of the family that continued into the 1960s in the United States, when the tremendous change in marriage and the family began to take place, as was reflected in the television series "Father Knows Best", "Ozzie and Harriet," and "Leave It To Beaver."

The second important change, the cult of female purity," had a different source. Before the industrial revolution and the advent of the Enlightenment, parents had ways of curtailing the sexual instincts of their children. This became much more difficult now as reflected by the sharp increase in the rate of out-of-wedlock children, which confirmed the worst fears of the middle and upper classes that personal freedom and romantic love could get out of hand. As one student of the family (again Stephanie Coontz) put it:

> "Central to this internal moral order was an unprecedented emphasis on female purity and chastity. Individuals whose parents and grandparents had blithely participated in such customs as bundling, kissing games, or nighttime courting visits now denounced these practices as scandalous. They also condemned the traditional rural practice of a couple only marrying after a woman got pregnant. . . .The older view that women had to be controlled because they were inherently more passionate and more prone to moral and sexual error, was replaced by the idea that women were asexual beings who would not respond to sexual overtures unless they had been drugged or deprived from an early age. . . .Where women had once been snares of the devil, they were now viewed as sexual innocents whose purity should inspire all

decent men to control their own sexual impulses and base appetites."

The conflict between these competing considerations and how they were imperfectly reconciled, led to the incredible turn that took place during the Victorian era. But it did not have the effect of bringing husbands and wives closer together, in the way that the romantic model of marriage suggested it would. As one student of the family (again Stephanie Coontz) put it;

"Despite society's abstract glorification of romance and married love, the day-to-day experience of marital intimacy was still quite circumscribed compared to standards that would prevail in the twentieth century. . . . Only when those limits were overcome did people discover just how thin a crust separated Victorian marital ideals from an explosion of new expectations about love, gender roles and marriage."

The inadequate accommodation worked out in the Victorian age between these competing considerations also created considerable emotional problems for middle class and upper class women, as was attested to by the fact that so many of Freud's female patients (and this was true of his fellow practitioners as well) came to him with what he labeled hysteria (derived from the Greek word for womb) as a result of the effects of sexual suppression they were required to experience, and it was common practice for physicians to massage their patient's pelvic areas, thereby bringing them to an orgasm, as part of their treatment. It was not until the "sexual revolution" that took place in the 20th century that this problem was addressed.

Our story is still not complete. To complete it, it is necessary to add two last things. As we have seen, the 18th and 19th centuries brought about a dramatic and unprecedented change in the makeup of the family. This was facilitated by the increased emphasis on personal autonomy (with what became characterized as "affective individualism"), which led to the much warmer personal relations between husbands and wives and between parents and children. This, in turn, had the effect of walling off what was increasingly referred to as the "nuclear family" from either influence or support from kin, community, the church or the state.

Contrary to what is normally the case, however, the historical developments that I have summarized were not linear in nature, as was the case, for example, with transportation. (Once the automobile was invented, we did not ever go back to the horse and buggy.) The same was not true, however, when it came to the tremendous changes that took place in the 18th century that led to the development of what we now refer to as romantic marriage. On the contrary, the growing individualism and permissiveness that characterized this period was both preceded by and followed, in the 17th and 19th centuries, by a strong revival of moral reform, paternal authority and sexual repression. As a result, and notwithstanding the turn to romantic marriage, until at least the early part of the 20th century, ours remained clearly a patriarchal society based on the God-given principle of hierarchy, deference, and obedience. And in that world, men ruled. Thus, although we have forgotten this, it was not until 1920 that women in the United States got the right to vote.

The second thing I must refer to in order to complete the story is the industrial revolution. I have already indicated one of the effects it had on the evolution of marriage and the family as we know it today, which was that it led to the emancipation of children from the control of their parents and family when it came to the choice of mate. But it had an equally important effect, one which we are generally not aware of.

Prior to the industrial revolution, the family was more than the primary economic unit. It was the nerve center of literally all of the family's life and activities. Not just where children were born and emotional needs were met, but also where such life activities as work, education, religion and security were provided. In an important sense, with the advent of the industrial revolution literally all of these activities were removed from the family and now supplied by outside agencies.

That, in and of itself, was not the problem. The problem, as literally all commentators of the scene have insisted, is that the world we were left with by the industrial revolution, and that we now live in, is an impersonal, anonymous, individualistic, and alienated one. To be sure, we have learned to get around and function in that world. (The whole purpose of what we call education today is to prepare us to do that.) But, in an important sense, it is an unreal world. It is a world in which we are assigned a number (our social security number) before we are even given a name, a number that will follow us, and by which we will be identified, throughout our entire life. As one student of the family (Christopher Lasch) put it, the "household", which was now referred to as the "home", had become simply "a haven in a heartless world", the private world of our family to which we retreated to escape the larger, increasingly impersonal world in which we lived.

This is critical. All social instruments (and the family is a social instrument) are supported by the functions they perform. If they didn't have any social functions, they would lose their importance, wither away and die. To be sure, marriage and the family still serve social functions today, if only limited ones. They are the setting in which we have children and form close personal relationships. However, as is evidenced by how often they break up, without all of the other social functions they performed, and that supported them in the past, they are more fragile and far more difficult to maintain. This is what led to the crisis in marriage and the family that we witnessed in the second half of the 20th century. The terrible irony is that it has left marriage and the family most vulnerable when it is most needed.

CHAPTER 17

FROM YOKE MATES
TO SOUL MATES

We used to be two. Now we are one. No, you are still two.

As I noted in the previous chapter, the advent of romantic, or companionate, marriage introduced the idea that though husbands and wives were different, and had different roles (separate spheres), they nevertheless complimented one another. As one student of the family (again Stephanie Coontz) put it:

> "The husband, once the supervisor of the labor
> force, came to be seen as the person who, by himself,
> provided for the family. The wife's role was redefined
> to focus on her emotional and moral contributions
> to family life rather than her economic inputs. The
> husband was the family's economic motor, and the
> wife its sentimental core . . . The new theory of gender
> difference divided humanity into two distinct sets
> of human traits. The male sphere encompassed the
> rational and active ideal, while females represented
> the humanitarian and compassionate aspects of life.
> When these two spheres were brought together in

marriage, they produced a perfect, well-rounded whole."

In Stephanie Coontz' terms, husbands and wives went from "yoke mates" to "soul mates." In the past they had been, and remained, two separate people who preceded together and worked together, side by side. Now in keeping with the romantic idea that each of them represented the missing half of the other, their union, which reunited them, represented a perfect fit, and they proceeded together as one.

With that in mind, I am going to quote from one last wedding announcement, one which combines all of the elements that I have referred to—love at first sight, common interests, and soul mates who were destined to meet one another.

"The couple, lovers of all things shellfish, met . . . at an Oysterfest in Piedmont Park, Atlanta. 'When I noticed this tall, handsome, dark-haired guy looking my way, I asked a girlfriend if she knew who he was' Ms. . . . said. 'Then to my complete mortification, my girlfriend marched right up to him and told him that I thought he was cute'."

"A few days after that, M. . . . received a Facebook message from Mr. . . . beginning with the words 'Hey, I think we met at the Oysterfest the other day."

"'I was stoked, just really excited,' Ms. . . . said." 'I had been thinking about him from the moment I first saw him."

"He asked her out to a seafood restaurant in Atlanta where they ordered a dozen oysters, and then a dozen more when they realized they had each made a pretty good catch."

'He's very endearing,' Ms. . . . said." 'He's the kind of guy who is a great listener, and remembers everything you tell him, which makes people around him feel very important'."

"Mr. . . . said that he and Ms. . . . . 'shared a similar sense of humor and a passion for trying new things'."

"'We had one great conversation after another, and things just clicked,' he said. 'I came to know her as a very hard worker, a very driven person with a great attitude toward life'."

"Before dinner ended, they realized that they had a lot more in common than their love of oysters."

"'I never really believed in fate until Ryan came along', she said."
"'But looking back now, it seems as if we were destined to be together'."

Unfortunately, like the premise upon which our notion of romantic love is based, the idea that husbands and wives are soul mates is nothing but an illusion. But, then, you don't need me to tell you that. You know it for yourself. As a husband and wife were two different people before they got married, so too they remain two different people after they get married. But it is even worse than that. All of their common values and common interests do not and could not change the fact that they are inherently different from one another—as I put it earlier, that they are mismatched. They are not the same. (If they were the same they wouldn't be mismatched.) They are different.

Before I get into that, however, I need to add one thing. Understandably, we are very sensitive to the suggestion that men and women are different. After all, that was the excuse given to support our patriarchic view of marriage since time immemorial, one which, as we saw, continued to prevail even after the advent of the concept of romantic marriage and the equality of the sexes upon which it was based. Nevertheless, if we are to understand the crisis in marriage that took place in the second half of the 20th century, which has resulted in the fact that almost one half of all first marriages in the United States today will end in divorce, we have to accept and come to terms with those differences.

They are different, first, because all people are different. They have different personal characteristics or, as we would put it, different personalities. To be sure, this may not constitute a problem. That will be so if they complement one another, as is the case with many successful businesses, where one of the partners is "Mrs. Inside", who handles the day to day operation of the business, and the other is "Mr. Outside", who bring in the business. But, as we have already seen, their different emotional dispositions can become a problem if, as is the case with their different adaptive styles, they run into one another.

Second, they are different based on the cultural considerations which define what it is to be a man and a woman, a husband and a wife, in a given society at any particular time, and because, on that basis, they see themselves as being different. Today, more than one-half of all bachelor degrees granted in the United States are earned by woman. Is that because women are smarter than men? Maybe they are and maybe they are not. But that is not the reason why more women than men earn bachelor degrees today. It certainly does not explain why women earned such a small percentage of bachelor degrees a century ago. Rather, it has to do with the roles society assigned to men and women at that time and, in keeping with that, how women viewed themselves.

Third, men and women are constitutionally different, by which I mean that they have different chromosomes. Women have an xx and men have an xy. In fact, it is that later chromosome that makes them men. The point is that those chromosomes play themselves out in different ways. Thus, boys have a 20% higher rate of death in the first year of their lives than do girls. They are also five times more likely to be autistic. For their part, girls' fine motor coordination skills are generally better than boys, which accounts for the fact that their handwriting is generally better. And so it goes down the line.

Finally they are different because they are not "soul mates." They are different because they are men and women and because men and women are different. I don't want to be misunderstood here. This has nothing to do with the equality of the sexes. I am not talking about whether one is better or more valuable than the other, and I am offended by the suggestion. I am talking about the fact that, for a variety of reasons, men and women are simply different. For example, men are generally taller than women. So what? Thus, rather than bringing together two people who have a lot in common, as the parties' reliance on their common values and interests assume, the marriage between any two people, whether they be of the same sex or opposite sexes, necessarily brings together two people who are different and who have far less in common than they assume. Nor does it make any difference which of those four considerations account for this. The marriage between any two people brings together two different people.

Why am I making so much of this? What difference does it make? It makes all of the difference in the world, as we will see when we get to Part II, where we will address the question of whether you will go forward, get a divorce and end your marriage, or go back and address the problems in your marriage in an attempt to sustain it, and chose the second of those alternatives.

What I have been arguing is that at least one of the reasons unhappily married husbands and wives find themselves where they are is that they have allowed themselves to be taken in by the unrealistic fantasy upon which our view of romantic marriage is based. As we say, they have been guilty of sleeping at the switch. That is not meant as a criticism. How could it be if all they were doing was what they were brought up to do and what everyone they knew was doing. Nevertheless, if their inclination is to go back and address the problems in their marriage, it won't do to cling to that illusion. Rather, if there is any hope that they will be left with a marriage that meets their essential needs, they will first have to be realistic in terms of what they have a right to expect and not expect of their marriage. In fact, that is the principal message of this book. It is also the principal message of the companion book to this one, *A Common Sense, Practical Guide To Divorce*, except in that case the question will be what they have a right to expect and not expect of their divorce and of the agreement that will bring their marriage to an end.

CHAPTER 18

SUMMING UP

*You know far more than you realize. All that
you have to do is take stock of it.*

I told you that when you finished reading this book you would be in a position to make an assessment as to whether it was realistic to believe that you would be able to go back and successfully work on the problems in your marriage in aid of your deciding whether you should do that or whether you should go forward, get a divorce, and end it. I am about to get to that assessment. Before I do, however, I want to summarize what you have learned in aid of your being able to make that decision.

First. The idea that we had when we got married that we were "soul-mates", that caused us to believe that we would be leading one life together rather than two, was nothing but an illusion born of the emotions that so overwhelmed us at the time. But as all husbands and wives learn, those emotions are more short lived than they expected, and when their intensity diminishes, as inevitably it will, the fantasy that they inspired will as well.

Second. Since it is not possible for us to lead one life together, the most that we can do is lead parallel lives that come closer together and then move further apart as we proceed with our separate lives.

Third. Though we do not realize it at the time, we marry total strangers. That is because, though we think we know the person we are marrying very well, we don't. In many respects we don't really know them at all.

Fourth. The two of us are more than total strangers. We are also mismatched. The person we are marrying is different from us and we from them in so many ways. In some respects, we are the exact opposite.

Fifth. The fact that we are mismatched means that out relationship will never be one of perfect harmony. Rather, it will always be in a state of balanced-imbalance. How could it be otherwise when you will always be you and I will always be me?

Sixth. The disharmony that we are going to experience in our marriage is not generally something, like a sudden illness or a financial reversal, that will be introduced into our marriage at a later point in time. Since in most instances it will be the fact that we were mismatched when we got married, it will be something that was there from the very beginning.

Seventh. In most instances it will not be possible for us to solve the problems we will encounter in our marriage by eliminating those differences. Rather, our marriage will represent our ongoing act of negotiating those differences and attempting to accommodate ourselves to them. That is why our marriage relationship will always be somewhat in a state of balanced imbalance.

Eighth. As today is not the same as yesterday, tomorrow will not be the same as today. As a result, the problems that we will encounter in our marriage will not necessarily be the same from one day to the next. Rather, they will change over time.

Ninth. That being so, though there will be an ongoing theme in our marriage, it will not constitute one marriage. Since we will encounter somewhat different problems as our lives go forward, and since what is a problem today may not have been a problem yesterday or, if it was, not as serious a problem, our marriage will constitute successive marriages.

Tenth. Notwithstanding that, since our necessarily different personal dispositions and adaptive styles will always remain a constant in our marriage, we will have to deal with them in all of our successive marriages.

Eleventh. The fact that we will be able to negotiate our differences or accommodate ourselves to them at one stage in our marriage doesn't mean that we will necessarily be able to (or want to) do that at another stage in our marriage.

Finally, the monumental changes that have taken place in marriage and the family in the last several hundred years, most particularly the introduction of the concept of romantic marriage, have necessarily had a tremendous effect on how all of these factors will play out. When marriages were arranged, when they were motivated by practical considerations, or when others (parents, family, relatives or members of our community) had a large influence over us when it came to who we would marry, these factors were not as significant. However, when that decision is now ours alone, particularly when we make it based on the powerful but nevertheless fleeting feelings that so overwhelm us at the time and govern our decisions, as is the case today, those factors become far more significant.

I

So much of what I have said up to this point was in aid of someone who was in a relationship that might lead to marriage to be able to base his or her decision on a firmer footing than is generally the case today. But, at this point at least, it is irrelevant. That is because you already got married. That being the case, you are now faced with a very different question, namely, whether or not the two of you should go forward, get divorced and end your marriage, and that has added a new element to the equation. That is why my summary up to this point is incomplete. It told you why you don't feel that you can continue to hold on to your marriage. But it didn't tell you why you have been unable to let go of it. I now want to address that.

If I were to ask you to name the two most important things in your life, the two things you could not possibly live without, what would you name? It is unlikely that you would name the air that you breath or the structure of your life. That is because you just take them for granted. But that does not mean that they are any less important on that account. On the contrary, just the opposite is the case. Your marriage represents the structure of your life–the air that you breathe. In fact, toward the end of Chapter 16 (Romantic Marriage) I reinforced that when I referred to Christopher Lasch's suggestion that the home has now become "a haven in a heartless world", and the fact that the impersonal, anonymous, indifferent and alienated world that we have inherited, and that we now live in, "has left marriage and the family most vulnerable when it is most needed."

That is what is missing from the summary that I have given up until this point. My summary may indicate why you feel that you can no longer hold on. But it doesn't indicate why you are having so much difficulty letting go. That is the fact that, as I said, you did get married and, in doing that, proceeded to create a history for yourself and relationships that included your husband or wife, and perhaps children. And that history and those relationships now constitute the air that you breathe and the very structure of your life, which is why it has been and may still be so hard for you to let go. Now my summary is complete.

CHAPTER 19

THE ASSESSMENT

We are always required to make the decisions in our lives
with less than adequate information.

It is now time for the assessment that you are going to make. Though you have two choices, the assessment is really only about one of those choices, namely, whether it is realistic for you to believe, based on what you now know, that if you go back and work on the problems in your marriage, you will be left with a marriage that meets your essential needs? I have put it that way for a reason. If you decide that it is unrealistic for you to believe that you will be able to do that, you will be left with only one choice, which is to go forward, get a divorce and end your marriage. To be sure, you have a third choice. You could just stay where you are, as you have done up to this point, and do nothing. But that will not solve your problem. It will just leave you where you now are, which is nowhere. Worse, more often than not it will only be to postpone the decision or leave it to your husband or wife to surprise you and make the decision for you, neither of which is very attractive.

Admittedly, you may still not be prepared to address the problem. As was the case when you started out, you may feel that you still do not have enough information to do that and are therefore still unsure.

What would make you feel more secure? If you knew exactly how it would turn out if you made the decision to go forward, get a divorce and end the marriage, or to go back and work on the problems in the marriage.

Unfortunately, you can't know that. To know that you would need a crystal ball. That is what it means to say that we are always required to make the decisions in our lives with less than adequate information. Nevertheless, I believe that I have given you all of the information you need to make that decision. I would certainly hope that you understand far better than you did before you started to read this book how and why you got to where you now are. Thus, if you are still struggling with that decision, the problem isn't that you do not have enough information. The problem is your inability to act on it.

Obviously, I can't make that decision for you. But, hopefully, I can help you do that. That is the purpose of the assessment that I want you to make. That assessment is not really to choose between the two options you have, namely, to go forward, get a divorce and end your marriage, or to go back, get some professional help and attempt to sustain it. It is really just to decide whether or not you will choose the second of those two choices.

How should you make that decision. I am going to argue that, when all is said and done, that is dependent upon the issue I raised at the conclusion of Chapter 12 when I asked whether your husband or wife was basically a decent person. To be sure, we all have our faults, just as we all have our limitations. But that does not mean that we are not basically decent people. Or is your husband (or wife) someone who you basically do not like.

This is critical. In fact, it is the litmus test. As I will argue, people are who they are. They don't change. They don't change for two reasons. The first is that, in most instance at least, they are very happy being who they are. The second is that they do not know how to change any more than they know how to grow two more inches in height. Thus, since you get what you see, the question is whether you really want to spend the rest of your life married to someone who you basically do not like–in the terms that I have put it, someone who you do not believe is basically a decent person. All that it is necessary to do is ask that question. What kind of life would that be?

It is very different, however, if your feel that your husband or wife is basically a decent person. To be sure, your hurt and anger may not permit you to answer that question in a positive way. But if you are no longer as hurt and angry as you now are, you may be able to see your husband or wife more realistically–the positive as well as the negative. That is because good things will again go on between the two of you. Our feelings toward one another are always a by-product of what goes on between us. That is why the first and foremost question is whether you are married to someone who you feel is basically a decent person. To be sure, once you get past that first question, there is a second and equally important one. Let me turn to that.

If you decide to go back and work on the problems in your marriage, it is critical that you be realistic in terms of what you can and cannot expect. As I will put it in Chapter 23, one cannot expect perfect solutions to imperfect problems. What we refer to as marriage counseling is not a magic elixir that can change a frog into Prince Charming. A frog is always going to remain what he is, a frog, and you must be willing to accept that. If you can't, there is no point in going back and attempting to work on the problems in your marriage. That is why the question of whether your husband or wife is basically a decent person is the litmus test.

Each of us has what I have described as an adaptive style that we employ in dealing with the challenges and problems that we are confronted with in our lives. I have referred to it as an adaptive style. You might also think of it as a defense mechanism. That is how we attempt to defend ourselves against those problems and challenges.

We see people employ these defense mechanisms all of the time. We even have names for them. Thus, we will say of someone that he is anxious, that he is compulsive or that he has an anal personality. Or, in other cases, we will say that he lives by the maxim that you should never put off for tomorrow something that you can put off for the following day. These, as I said, are their adaptive styles. That is not the problem. The problem is that their adaptive style is running interference with your adaptive style. The problem is that they will never be willing to give up their adaptive style, any more than you will be willing to give up yours. (It would be like asking you to shrink two inches.) If it comes down to that, they would rather go down in flames than do that.

But if your wife (or husband) is overly anxious, and it is driving you crazy because she is trying to make you as anxious as she is, if the two of you go into marriage counselling, can't she be shown the error of her ways? The answer is no. An objective third person may know that your wife (or husband) is anxious because she is basically an anxious person. But from your wife's standpoint she is anxious because she has good reason to be. There are always potential dangers waiting for us just around the corner, and it is not her problem that she sees them and you don't. Nor will you ever be able to prove to her that it is not possible for them to occur–that this is just something that she is imagining or making up in her head. For her it is as real as the nose on her face.

This was dramatically brought home to me in the course of a mediation I conducted. When I concluded a mediation, I always prepared a draft of the couple's proposed agreement and sent it to each of them. It didn't look like a draft but I always referred to it as that to make it clear that when we next met they were not going to sign it. My practice was to go over the draft with them, page by page and paragraph by paragraph, to make sure that each of them understood it, that it accurately reflected their understanding, to answer any questions they had, and to make whatever changes were required. I then put the agreement into final form and again sent a copy of it to each of them, at which point, unless there were further changes that had to be made, the two of them would come in and sign it.

When I started to go over the agreement with a couple at that first meeting, I always told them that, when they received the final agreement, it would not be necessary for them to go over it page by page, paragraph by paragraph, as they no doubt had when it came to the draft of the agreement that I had sent to them. That was because their final agreement was going to be accompanied by a letter in which I would indicate every change that had been made to that draft agreement. All that they would have to do is read my letter and go to the page and paragraph in question and check the change that I had refereed to. I was always proud of that procedure as it simplified things for the couple with whom I was working.

When I told the couple here what I intended to do, and why it would not be necessary for them to reread the entire agreement, the wife interjected and told me that she had not only read the draft of the agreement page by page and paragraph by paragraph, but word by word as well, and that it was her intention to do the same when it came to the final agreement that I planned to send to her. Since this was none of my business, I did not respond to what the wife said.

When we met again, this time to sign the final agreement, the wife proudly informed me that she had reread it, as she said she would, and that she had found a mistake (a typographical error) in one word of the agreement. Why was she telling me that? She was giving me (and herself) proof that her adaptive style was not just a figment of her imagination. It was correct, and she was therefore right in rereading the final agreement page by page, paragraph by paragraph and word by word.

It has to be assumed that the wife here would not receive the same validation the next time, or the time after that, when she employed her adaptive style. Would that call into question her faith in it? Would you be able to point to that as proof that her adaptive style was as wasteful and maladaptive as you believed it to be? No. She would always be able to go back to the instance I just related where, in her mind at least, it was validated. That is why she would rather go down in flames than question her adaptive style.

That is why it makes no sense to go back and work on the problems in your marriage in the hope that your husband or wife will be willing or able to change what I have referred to as their adaptive style. They won't. Thus, if you are married to a woman who is anxious, if you stay married to her you will always be married to a woman who is anxious. That is what I mean when I say that, in making an assessment as to whether it makes sense to go back and attempt to work on the problems in your marriage, you must be realistic in terms of what you can expect and not expect. I am not suggesting that accommodations and compromises will not have to be made if you are going to successfully work on the problems in your marriage. They will. And if the two of you are able to do that, and you no longer see your husband or wife through the negative feelings that currently affect your view of them, if your husband or wife is what I have described as a basically decent person, you will be able to see them in a different, more positive light.

There are two other things that I need to add. The first is the distinction that I want to make between "the problems in your marriage" and "the problems that affect your marriage"—the problems that the two of you have to work on and the problems that your husband or wife has to work on. Obviously, if your husband or wife is an alcoholic or a drug addict, or has some other addiction, such as an addiction to gambling, that is something that is going to have a dramatic effect on your marriage. For most people it is not possible to live with someone who is addicted to alcohol, drugs or gambling. But it is not a problem in your marriage in the sense that the two of you are going to have to work on it. Your husband or wife is either going to work on it or not work on it. If they are willing and able to work on it, there will no longer be a problem that is affecting your marriage. If they are not, it will continue to affect your marriage. But it is not a problem in your marriage in the sense of being something that the two of you are going to have to work on together. (This is not to suggest that you may not have to support your husband in his attempt to deal with his problem. It is just to make the distinction between these two types of problems.) Thus, the only decision that you will have to make is whether you will go forward and end the marriage if your husband or wife is not willing or able to deal with their problem.

The second concerns those things that your husband or wife may not have any control over, such as a severe emotional problem. Again, in my terms, though this will certainly have an effect on your marriage, it is not a problem in your marriage in the sense that the two of you can work on it. And it may be something that is not going to go away.

The point is that these are things that you have to consider in making your assessment. That is what I mean when I say that you have to be realistic. That means being willing and able to stare the problem in the face. If you have not done that up to this point, that is because you were afraid that doing so would force you to do something that you did not want to do, which was to go forward, get a divorce and end your marriage. That is your decision. But if you are not willing or able to stare the problem in the face, you must know that you have not solved your problem. You are just condemning yourself to more of the same.

There is an exception to what I have just said. The way I have presented the problem suggests that you only have two choices, either to go forward or to go back. Otherwise you will just be left where you are. I now want to stand corrected.

There are couples who lead what I have called parallel lives that, like railroad tracks, proceed in the same direction but never touch. Their parallel lives may not be as extreme as the couple I mentioned earlier who sat at a table in a restaurant having dinner together, across from my wife and I, who never made eye contact or spoke to one another the entire time. But though there is some interaction between the husband and wife I am thinking about (and I have in mind a particular couple), there is really no affection between them, and their relationship is based more on habit than anything else.

I am not talking about a couple who has been married for only 5 or 10 years. I am talking about a couple who has been married more than 40 years, whose children are grown and now on their own, and who are retired and living principally on their social security payments and retirement benefits. While their income may be limited, given their circumstances it is adequate, so long as they stay together. It will be very different, however, if they divorce and go their separate ways. Neither of them will be able to live in the future as they were able to live in the past.

To be sure, there are couples no younger than the couple I am describing who, when they divorce, will go on with their lives, which will include forming new, personal relationships. But unlike the wife in the previous story I told (whose husband I described as a poor excuse for a human being), who I had no doubt would grab hold of life and do that, the wife I am referring to here probably would not. It might not even occur to her. Both she and her husband are not likely either to go forward or to go back. They are going to stay just where they are and finish out their lives together. In fact, since neither of them is going to read this book, I have not included a discussion of them for their benefit. Thus, the only reason I have introduced them into the discussion is to complete the story. There are husbands and wives who will not choose either of the two alternatives I have posed.

Would the husband or wife here be making a mistake. Aside from the fact that it would be extremely inappropriate for me to make judgements in other people's lives, how could I say that? Though the road is always unclear for those who opt to go forward and end their marriage, it has to be far less clear for a husband and wife such as this. How can they be faulted if they decide to leave well enough alone?

I want to conclude by returning to the assessment that you are going to make (if you are so inclined) as to whether you feel it is realistic for you to believe that you will be able to successfully work on the problems in your marriage.

Let us assume for the moment that you are both of the same mind here–you both want to attempt to do that. You are still not done. That is because, if you both so decide, there will be a second assessment, this one conducted by the person you turn to in an effort to do that. Having met with the two of you, does he (or she) feel that you are suitable candidates (that you will be successful) or does he feel that you would be wasting your time. After all, you don't want to waste your time. That second assessment is therefore important. I will get to it in Part II.

PART II

Sustaining the Marriage

CHAPTER 20

THE CURRENT ROADMAP

If you want to get to a predetermined destination,
you will have to follow the right roadmap

You have made the assessment and, in the terms that I posed it in Chapter 19, have come to the conclusion that, based upon what you now know, it is realistic to believe that if you go back and work on the problems in your marriage, there is a good chance that you will be left with a marriage that meets your essential needs. And that is what you want to do. The only question is how you are going to go about doing that.

The principal theme of this book (and this is true of its companion book as well) is that if you want to get to a predetermined destination, you will have to follow the right roadmap. You can't get to a predetermined destination in Georgia by following a roadmap of Virginia.

And that is the problem you are faced with. Almost one half of all marriages today in the United States will end in divorce. In the vast majority of instances, one or both of the parties sought help in an effort to sustain their marriage. If they didn't succeed, there could only be one of two reasons. Either there was really little if any chance that they would succeed or, in the terms that I put it, they weren't following the right roadmap.

I want to assume that the first of those reasons would not be true in your case. You did not make your decision to go back and address the problems in your marriage by flipping a coin. You read this book and, in doing so, were left with a much better understanding than you previously had as to how and why, despite your high expectations, you came to the point where you now are. And it was on that basis that you made your decision. To be sure, nothing in life is certain. Nevertheless, it is reasonable for you to assume that if you get the right help—in the terms that I have put it, follow the right roadmap—and are realistic in terms of what you have a right to expect and not expect, you stand a good chance of succeeding.

I

That brings us to the critical question. What is the right roadmap? If the truth be told, there are as many different roadmaps as there are mental health professionals to whom you can turn for help. Nevertheless, there is a very strong family resemblance when it comes to most of them. That is because, despite their differences, they are all based on the very same basic assumptions. That being the case, I am going to refer to only one of them, that advanced by Dr. John Gottman in his book *The Seven Principles for Making Marriage Work*, and all page references are to that book. I am doing that for two reasons. First, because Dr. Gottman is a well-known and respected marriage counselor, and the author of many books on the subject. Second, and more important, because he claims that his conclusions are based on many years of scientific research. (P. 4) That is the roadmap that I am going to take up, and admittedly critique, in this chapter. In the following chapter I will propose a new, very different, roadmap.

I said that Dr, Gottman maintains that the validity of his analysis of the problems that husbands and wives currently have in sustaining their marriages, and the basis for the roadmap he has created for them to follow in dealing with those problems, is based on scientific research (studies) which he and his colleagues conducted over many decades, that enabled him to predict, "with great precision, whether a couple will stay happily married or lose their way after listening to them interact for as little as fifteen minutes." (P. 2) That being the case, the first order of business is to examine those studies and the conclusions he drew from them. I will tell you in advance that I am going to argue that none of those studies qualify as scientific studies and that none of them could possibly be used to justify the conclusions Dr. Gottman drew from them. But I am going to go further. I am going to argue that all that Dr. Gottman has performed is a pulling a rabbit out of the hat trick. As they say, the hand is quicker than the eye.

In that regard, and to set the stage for my argument that Dr. Guttman's claimed scientific studies were anything but that, I am going to quote from his first reference to one of them. (P. 2, 3)

> "Why is marriage so tough at times? Why do some lifelong relationship click while others just tick away like a timebomb? And how can you prevent a marriage from going bad—or rescue one that is already in trouble?
>
> Predicting divorce makes for great headlines, but sometimes the statistics can be confusing . . . Our studies predict divorce over a much shorter time frame. For example, in a study of 130 newlywed couples, we determined which fifteen of them would divorce over the next seven years based on our analysis of their interactions. In fact, seventeen couples divorced (including our fifteen), making our prediction rate for the study 98 percent." (P. 2, 3)

Without doubt, that is a very impressive prediction rate. And I have no doubt that those who have read Dr. Gottman's book (and he sold more than a million copies of it) came away having every confidence in him. But that is not the issue. Were his predictions based, as he would have us believe, on a scientific study that he conducted. Since Dr. Gottman never told us what was the basis for his prediction, we will never know. (For all we know, he could have picked the fifteen couples out of a hat.) But, as I will demonstrate, we don't have to know.

A scientific experiment is a controlled experiment. That is why all scientific experiments are performed in a laboratory where the person conducting the experiment can control the factors at play. How can he determine whether Factor A was the cause of the result if Factors B, C and D were also at play? He can't. That is why a scientist conducts the study in an environment that does not contain Factors B, C, or D.

Consider the couples in the study that Dr. Gottman conducted. All that he told us about them was that they were newlyweds. What is a newlywed? Is it someone who was married yesterday, within the last year, two years or five years ago? Dr. Gottman never told us. But from other things that he said in his book we can assume that by a newlywed he meant a couple who had been married for a year or less. We wouldn't refer to a couple who had been married for 4 years or 5 years as a newlywed couple.

Were the 130 couples picked at random? Were all or any of them couples who had already sought professional help for the problems in their marriage? Did any of them feel that they were having problems in their marriage? Did Dr. Gottman even ask them any of those questions? In fact, did Dr. Gottman know anything at all about them? The answer is no.

It has to be assumed that his evaluations of their "interactions" was not a positive one. It was not all smiles, hugs and kisses. There was at least some negativity in them. If that was the case now, when they were still newlyweds, it wouldn't be too hard to imagine what it would be over the next seven years, if they were still married. The dice were loaded in favor of their getting a divorce. In fact, they were so loaded that my 14 year old grandson could have picked them out.

But that is not the issue. Remember the question that Dr. Gottman posed that his scientific experiment was supposed to answer. "Why do some lifelong relationships click while others just tick away like a timebomb? And how can you prevent a marriage from going bad—or rescue one that is already in trouble?" What did Dr. Gottman and his colleagues learn from this "scientific experiment" that would enable them to answer that question, let alone serve as the basis for the roadmap that he was recommending that husbands and wives who were having problems in their marriage should follow? It is a rhetorical question. Since he didn't ask any of the 130 couples who were the basis of this study a single question, the answer is that he didn't learn anything.

But I don't want to leave it at that. I want to address it from two other angles. You will accept that if you had attended their wedding, it would have been all smiles, hugs and kisses—that, unlike now, everything would have been in place—and that if Dr. Gottman was also a guest, he would never have predicted that they would get divorced in the next seven years. On what possible basis could he have made that prediction? On none.

But isn't that the question that any scientific experiment that he conducted should have been designed to answer. Certainly that was what I was trying to do in Part I of this book when I devoted more than one hundred pages to enumerating all of the factors that would or might have an influence on their marriage going forward.

This brings me to the second angle that I want to view his supposed scientific experiment from. As Dr. Gottman acknowledged (P. 3), over a 40 year period almost 50% of all married couples in the United States will divorce. In the study in question, he identified 15 of the 17 who would divorce within the next seven years. That is what gave him a prediction rate of 98%. But what about the other 113 couples? Do any of us believe that Dr. Gottman's prediction rate when it came to which of those other 113 couples would divorce before their

40th wedding anniversary would be 98%? Would he even suggest that? It is a rhetorical question.

But that doesn't detract from his astonishing 98% prediction rate when it came to the study of those 130 newlywed couples . Yes it does. It makes a farce of his prediction. What was the basis for Dr, Gottman's prediction. He told us. As he said, it was "based on our analysis of their interactions."(P. 3) These were newlyweds. That being the case, it would be reasonable to assume that they were still at least somewhat under the sway of "being in love", and their interaction should have reflected that. Obviously, it didn't. On the contrary, it reflected that, unlike the other couples in the study, they had already wandered off into troubled waters.

That brings us to the other 113 couples. To be sure, they weren't going to divorce in the next seven years. But that didn't mean that they wouldn't divorce. We know that a very great percentage of them would. Dr. Gottman acknowledged that. It is not without significance that Dr. Gottman did not make any prediction when it came to the other 113 couples. How could he? Unlike the 15 couples that he predicted would divorce within the next seven years, at that point there was nothing for him to go on when it came to the other 113 couples.

This is critical. Dr. Gottman and his associates were not conducting the experiments that they did over several decades out of idle curiosity, in this case to enable them to make a prediction as to whether a particular married couple would or would not divorce in that 40 year period. They were conducting those experiments to answer the very important question that Dr. Gottman posed in his book, and that I highlighted in the hope that what they learned would improve the chances of a married couple to sustain their marriage. What did their experiment teach them? Nothing. How could it when they didn't know anything about the couples involved let alone ask them a single question.

As I said, Dr. Gottman submitted all of this as representing the result of scientific studies that he and his colleagues conducted over decades, not only as proof of his ability to make predictions when it came to the couples who came to him for help but also to validate his therapeutic methodology. I hope that I have sufficiently answered the first of those claims. It is now time for me to address the second.

II

This brings me to the second problem, namely, the methodology that Dr. Gottman and most of the other mental health professionals who husbands and wives turn to for help currently employ. In my terms, it is a methodology that does not include all of the relevant factors at play when it comes to marriage today and, more importantly, the problems that husbands and wives are having in sustaining their marriage. If that is the case (and it is the burden of this book to establish that), it will not be possible for them to be of help to the husbands and wives who come to them with the problems that they are having in their marriage.

What is wrong with the roadmap which they are presently following? The fact that it leaves out so many of the relevant factors that are at play in marriage today that were not factors (or at least not as important factors) in the past. The first and most important is the different emotional dispositions and adaptive styles of the parties, which I summarized in Chapter 14. The second is the incredible changes in marriage itself, and in our attitude toward it, that we have witnessed in the last several hundred years, which I summarized in Chapters 16 and 17. The roadmap which Dr. Guttman recommends, and the advice that he gives on the basis of it, proceed as if all of this had never occurred. And this is true of most of the other mental health professionals who follow the same roadmap.

While this failure is critical when it comes to that roadmap, because I do not want to belabor the point, I will only give two examples of this. But I could give many more.

The first has to do with an issue that I already raised in Chapter 14, namely sex. If I have already addressed it, why am I bringing it up again? Because, while those who, like Dr. Gottman, follow the current roadmap either make no reference to the differences in the emotional dispositions of husbands and wives, let alone address them, it is far more difficult to ignore them when it comes to sex. That is because the parties will put the issue on the table even if the mental health professional with whom they are working will be inclined to let sleeping dogs lie.

Is this as much of a problem as I am suggesting? It must be. After all, Dr, Gottman does not refer to it just in passing. On the contrary, he devotes over 10 pages to it. As he says, "No area of a couple's life offers more potential for embarrassment, hurt, and rejection than their sexual relationship." (P. 222) And the problem is always the same. For the husband it is that his wife is rarely interested in having sexual relations. For the wife it is that having sexual relations is all that her husband is interested in.

What is Dr. Guttman's solution to this problem? He really doesn't have one. That is because the current roadmap that he is following does not admit that husbands and wives can be constitutionally different, and to go down that road (to admit that possibility) could be very dangerous. After all, the claimed difference between men and women was responsible for the fact that women were not granted the right to vote in the United States until 1920. So Dr. Gottman's solution to the problem is to suggest that they "Learn to talk to each other about sex in a way that lets each partner feel safe." (P. 224). Did he really say that? Was that really his solution? Yes.

What is going on here? Neither Dr. Gottman nor any other mental health professional has ever suggested that sex offered more potential for embarrassment, hurt and rejection in a couple's lives than their sexual relationship before they married. If that was not the case then, why is it the case now? That is what I was referring to when I said that Dr. Gottman was following the wrong roadmap. It didn't incorporate literally any of the considerations that I documented in such detail in Part I of this book. As I pointed out there, contrary to what Plato argued in the Symposium, men and women were never joined together as one. They always had different emotional dispositions and adaptive styles, and following a roadmap that does not reflect that will not bring them to where they want to get.

Ironically, Dr. Gottman acknowledges the truth of what I have just said. Thus, after pointing to new techniques that have been developed both for improving couples therapy and preventing relationship problems, he adds, "But despite the gradual increase in useful and helpful approaches, the majority of marriage counselors are offering treatment that does not get to the heart of what makes a long-term relationship last." (P. 10) That is all well and good. But, in the terms that I have defined the debate, in using what I have characterized as the wrong roadmap, Dr. Gottman only contributes to the problem.

III

There is one last serious problem with the roadmap that Dr. Guttman is recommending. In many ways it is the most serious problem of all. As I have argued over and over again in this book, it is the fact that we have romanticized marriage.

Although I am sure he is not aware of this, Dr. Gottman subscribes to and affirms all of the misguided assumptions and unrealistic expectations that support the fantasy of romantic marriage. In fact, he is the Preacher in Chief when it comes to romantic love.

And therein lies the problem. Over and over again Dr. Gottman has the bad habit of romanticizing what is already far too romanticized. In doing that, he adds fuel to the fire, first, by sending husbands and wives off in the wrong direction and, second, by holding out unrealistic expectations.

Because he is a romanticist when it comes to marriage, the vision that he holds out to husbands and wives who are experiencing problems in their marriage is the possibility that they will be able to return to the emotional state they originally were in before they got married, one that "fuels the romance, passion, and great sex that we all hope marriage will provide." (P. 51) It makes no difference that that "emotional state" was a short lived illusion. It makes no difference that it held out unrealistic levels of expectation that were inevitably followed by equivalent levels of disappointment. It makes no difference that, as I noted earlier, the result was that "the majority of marriage counselors are offering treatment that does not get to the heart of what makes a long-term relationship last." (P. 10) As a romanticist, every love story must end with the words, "and they lived happily ever after."

To be sure, as Dr. Gottman acknowledged, while those were the closing words of every love story, they were not the closing words of every marriage. How could they be if so many husbands and wives who started out with such high hopes and expectations ended up in his office? How could they be when, despite the professional help they received, so many of those marriages ended in divorce.

It made no difference. As I said, Dr. Gottman is the Preacher in Chief of romantic marriage and there is literally not a page in his book where he does not beat the drum of romantic love. He refers to the place where he conducts his experiments as a "love lab." (P. 1) He refers to the questionnaire that he has a couple complete to test the strength of their marriage as a "Love Maps Questionnaire." (P. 56) He refers to the game that he has the couple play to test how well they know each other as "The Love Map 20 Questions Game." (P. 56) As I said, it is love, love, love from beginning to end.

But it is worse than that. With very rare exception, Dr. Gottman does not recognize, let alone address, any of the considerations I enumerated, in Part I that have contributed to the problems that husbands and wives today are encountering in their marriage, despite the fact that they have left us confronted with the reality that almost one-half of all marriages in the United States today (and this applies to second and third marriages as well) will end in divorce.

To be sure, I am not suggesting that the new roadmap I am going to propose will be able to eliminate all of those considerations. That would be to engage in a fantasy as unrealistic as the one that Dr. Gottman endorses. But, unlike the current roadmap that Dr. Gottman recommends, it does realistically take those considerations into account.

CHAPTER 21

THE NEW ROADMAP

*If you want to get to a different destination, you
will have to follow a different roadmap*

I have shown you the current roadmap. It is now time to outline the new roadmap that I am proposing.

First. The roadmap that I am proposing is not one grounded in a romantic fantasy that ends "and they all lived happily ever after." To be sure, the high that those who marry experience when they are in the thralls of that fantasy is no doubt the most exhilarating one they will ever experience. But that artificially induced high does not and cannot last.

Second. The roadmap that I am proposing takes into account and, more importantly, accepts the limitations in the undertaking. As I have argued, the problems you are experiencing in your marriage are largely a function of two things. One is the fact that, whether your marriage is an opposite sex or a same sex marriage, the two of you came to it with different emotional dispositions. The other is that the two of you came to it with different adaptive styles. Moreover, one of the principal reasons that you are having problems in your marriage is that those different emotional dispositions and adaptive styles are rubbing up against one another. While the roadmap that I am proposing will hopefully reduce the friction that is created when they do, it cannot eliminate it. Nor can either of you change your emotional dispositions or adaptive styles. They are in your DNA. (I will take that up in more detail in Chapter 23, when I discuss the inherent limitations in the undertaking.)

That being the case, the approach that the roadmap I am proposing will take will not be to attempt to eliminate your different emotional dispositions and adaptive styles. As I said, that is not possible. It will be to explore whether it will be possible for you to be more conscious of the effect they are having on your marriage (relationship) in the hope that the two of you will be better able to control them. Again, I am not saying that being more aware of the effect that they are having on your marriage will necessarily enable you to do that. All that I am saying is that, as your experience has taught you, there is no chance that you will be able to control them more effectively if you are not consciously aware of them and the effect that they are having on your marriage.

Third. Unlike the current roadmap that I described in the last chapter, there will be no quizzes to take or games to play to test and determine your love for one another and whether it has increased as a result of the counseling you are receiving. The purpose of the roadmap that I am proposing is not to revive the fantasy that induced you to marry. It is to improve your marriage by putting it on a sounder and more realistic basis.

I appreciate that there will be those who will accuse my approach to the problems you are experiencing in your marriage as being very unromantic. They will say that I have taken all of the life out of your marriage. They will say that I have reduced it to materialistic determinism—to the advice I would give to someone who was trying to save a failing business.

I would take strong exception to that. You will grant me that you cannot love someone who you do not know. You will further grant me that you cannot really know someone if you have only had a half-hours conversation with them, or even a longer one over dinner. Finally, you will grant me that you cannot love someone unless you see them. Looking at a picture of them is not seeing them. It is only seeing a picture of them. And the same is true if your picture of them is distorted by the artificial haze of romantic love. To be sure, that picture is incredibly powerful. But, as you have learned, it is also very distorted.

But it is worse than that, much worse. We do not normally prioritize "being in love" with someone over "loving" someone. After all, we do not say that we are in love with our children or that we are in love with the work that we do. We say that we love our children and the work that we do. Do we feel that we have diminished our children or the work that we do on that account? It is a rhetorical question. But I will go further. Is it any less a compliment to say that I have a great deal of respect or admiration for someone than it is to say that I love them? I would argue that it is just the other way around.

And what is true when it comes everything else in our lives is also true of our marriage. I cannot think of a greater compliment that I could pay my wife than to say that I love her. That is because I am making a statement about how I view her, not about some illusion I have of her. My point is that if you follow the roadmap that I am proposing, and if you find that it was helpful, it will not leave you with a diminished marriage. On the contrary, it will leave you with an enhanced marriage. What proof will you have of that? The fact that you will consider yourself to be very lucky.

There is one last thing that I want to say about the new roadmap I am proposing. Unlike the current roadmap that most mental health professionals employ, it is not based on what I have referred to as a Garden of Eden cosmology. In other words, it does not attribute the problems in a couple's marriage to the misconduct of one of them—as we have traditionally put it, to someone's fault. (If he or she had not been guilty of such misconduct, they would have lived "happily ever after.") Rather it insists that the problem is inherent in the undertaking—in this case, attributable to all the factors and considerations that I enumerated in such detail in Part I.

To be sure, one or both of the parties may not have always acted as thoughtfully as they could have. They might even have added to the problem in other ways as well. After all, none of us is perfect. But as our experience tells us, being perfect is not a precondition for a marriage to go the distance. If it were, no marriage could possibly make it.

That is why the principal mission of this book has been to put a lie to all of the nonsense that has traditionally been invoked to explain divorce, and to substitute for it what will hopefully be a better, more useful understanding.

Why, then, do marriages today so often not go the distance. Because what the roadmap that most mental health professionals today follow does not take into account is that the problem comes with the territory. All that you have to do to see this is to contrast the new roadmap that I am proposing with the one that mental health professionals like Dr. Gottman are currently following. Which of those roadmaps would you label as pie in the sky and which would you label as telling it as it is?

Almost the entire Part I of this book, running to more than 100 pages, was devoted to recounting in great detail the very dramatic changes that have taken place in society in the last 300 to 350 years that have impacted on marriage and the family today. I also enumerated in as great detail the differences between husbands and wives, and in all partners in a marriage, that also have to be factored into the equation in order to understand marriage at the present time. But, as I underscored in my discussion of the roadmap that Dr. Gottman would have you follow, he did not take into account even one of those factors. Worse, and as I also underscored, from beginning to end his book represents an endorsement of the romantic vision of marriage which has brough us to where we are today.

This brings me back to the new roadmap that I am proposing. Am I suggesting that following it will guarantee that you will live "happily ever after." Of course not. That is nonsense. Like Dr. Gottman, I cannot change all of the influences and considerations that have come into play in the last several hundred years that have impacted on marriage today. But, unlike the current roadmap that Dr. Gottman and most of his colleagues presently follow, the new one that I am proposing takes them into account.

I

There are two last issues that I need to address. I have already devoted some time and attention to the fact that, whether it is a same sex marriage or an opposite sex marriage, any two people will have somewhat different emotional dispositions and adaptive styles, and that this will necessarily impact on their marriage.

But I have raised another issue as well, and that is whether men and women are inherently different. I will now pose it in somewhat different terms. Are they or are they not cut from the same cloth?

If men and women (really any two people) are cut from the same cloth, they are basically the same. In other words, they are well matched. However, if they are not cut from the same cloth, and particularly if they are cut from different cloth, they are or may be inherently different and, therefore, not well matched. Which is it?

I have taken the position that they are not cut from the same cloth--that they are mismatched. What is Dr. Gottman's position? I am not sure. To be more precise, I do not think that he is. Thus, on page 19 he announces, in bold letters, "So men and women come from the same planet after all"—in my terms, that they are cut from the same cloth. But in the next breath, on page 42, he insists, again in bold letters, that based on our "evolutionary heritage", "Men and Women Really Are Different."

This is not simply an academic question. Particularly in the context here, it has very practical implications. Again, since I do not want to belabor the point, I will just bring up one.

As I have already noted, Dr. Gottman acknowledged that one of the problems that husbands and wives who turn to mental health professionals for help commonly come in complaining about is the frequency of their intimate sexual relations. As he said,

> "No area of a couple's life offers more potential for embarrassment, hurt, and rejection than their sexual relationship. . . . In the most common scenario, the

husband desires sex significantly more than the wife."
(P. 222)

As I have argued, this was not a problem before they got married. But it is now, the husband claiming that his wife never wants to engage in sex and his wife complaining that that is all that her husband ever wants to engage in.

I don't think that there is any question that this is an issue in a great many marriages. Dr. Guttman admitted it was. The question is what caused it. I would argue that Dr, Gottman is of two minds about this. To complicate this even more, though he is of one mind when it comes to the solution, he is of two minds when it comes to the cause.

Let us start with the solution. For Dr. Gottman it is based on the fact that men and women approach the issue from different points of view. A man wants to have sex; a woman wants to make love. I am admittedly simplifying this a bit. The woman in question may not even want to make love. But that will get us nowhere and, understandably, Dr. Gottman does not proceed on that assumption. So for him the solution is in how a husband approaches his wife. It should not be abruptly. It should be romantically.

This would not be such a significant issue if the question was simply whether men and women have different views when it comes to sex. As I argued earlier, what makes it a larger issue is the fact that, though their attitudes toward sex was very much the same before they married, it is very different now, after they have married. Before they married neither of them could get it fast enough or often enough. Now, however, it is very different.

The question I have raised is not just an academic one for another reason. It has significant implications beyond their sexual relations as well. After all, if men and women are inherently different, this will or may affect other aspects of their marriage, even if not as dramatically. Unfortunately, Dr. Gottman's discussion of the question is not very helpful when it comes to this. That is because, though he recognizes the difference between men and women, he refers to evolutionary events that took place in the very remote past that account for this, not the revolutionary events that took place only in the last couple of centuries. In fact, they are so long ago that it is as if they never took place.

The point is that if Plato was wrong in the Symposium when he claimed that men and women were originally as one, then they are not cut from the same cloth, and if that is the case it adds yet another consideration into the picture, namely, that they are inherently different. Unfortunately, that is not reflected in the current roadmap. It can't be. It is incompatible with the romantic view of marriage upon which that roadmap is grounded, namely, that the two of them are cut from the same cloth.

II

There is another critical difference in the current roadmap that Dr. Gottman is following and the new roadmap that I am proposing. The new roadmap that I am proposing is not grounded on the assumption that husbands and wives get divorced because they are not very happy in their marriage. It is grounded on the assumption that they get divorced because they are very unhappy in their marriage. Isn't that one and the same thing? No. Let me explain.

As I said, Dr. Gottman is a romanticist when it comes to marriage. As such, there is no in between. It is either one or the other, and he views his role to be to turn one (a very unhappy marriage) into the other (a very happy marriage). That is not the problem. The problem is that, being a romanticist, he sets a very high (I would say unrealistic) standard for himself. The yardstick that he uses to measure the state of a couple's marriage is the one that they used to measure it by when they got married, namely, whether it "fuels the romance, passion, and great sex that we all hope marriage will provide" (P. 51) –in the terms that I have just put it, whether it is a very happy marriage.

Thein lies the problem. The only time that the two of them were very happily married in Dr. Gottman's terms was when they were "in love." This is not to say that they do not still love one another.

They do. They are just no longer "in love" with one another in the sense that they were when they married. But that is still sufficient. In other words, husbands and wives who seek help in their marriage do not complain that they are no longer "in love" with one another. They don't think in those terms. Why would they when they love one another? They only feel that loss when the problems in their marriage have so overwhelmed one or both of them that it is no longer possible for them to love one another—in the terms that I have put it, when they are very unhappy in their marriage. In other words, there are three possible states, not just two. In the first they are both consciously aware that they are very happy in their marriage, in the second one or both of them is consciously aware that they are very unhappy in their marriage, and in the third it is not something that either of them thinks about (asks themselves). The point is that it is only someone in the second group (those who are very unhappy in their marriage) who either seeks help for the problems in their marriage or divorces because of them, not someone in the first or third group.

Why is this important? It is important in the sense of our having a better understanding of the problem that husbands and wives may be having in their marriage and what the object of someone who is trying to help them sustain their marriage should be. In the terms that I have put it, it is important when it comes to the roadmap that the mental health professional they turn to for help follows, the current one exemplified by Dr. Gottman or the new one that I am proposing.

Contrary to the romantic view of marriage that has been bequeathed to us, which is the basis of the roadmap that Dr. Gottman recommends, the standard of the roadmap that I am proposing is not one that meets the requirements of those in either the first group or the third group. It is only the lower one that is necessary to meet the requirements of those in the second group—in the terms that I have posed it, those who are very unhappy in their marriage. That being the case, the issue is whether following either the current roadmap or the new one that I am proposing will solve the problems (in my terms, the conflicts) that are causing one or both of the parties to be very unhappy in their marriage.

But Dr. Gottman's romanticized view of marriage isn't content with changing a very unhappy marriage into a happy one and to leave it at that. That is where his fantasy of romantic love enters the picture. As he says, he wants to go further and leave them with "a positive attitude (that) not only allows them to maintain but also to increase the sense of romance, play, fun, adventure, and learning together that are at the heart of any long lasting love affair." P. 4) As he says at another point, he wants to "divorce proof" their marriage. (P. 51) But how could he possibly do that? To do that he would have to know all of the things that will transpire in their lives in the future that could adversely affect their marriage as well as the resources that that they will or will not have to deal with them. Needless to say, he could not possibly know that. To know that he would need a crystal ball. As neither he nor they could possibly have known when they got married all of the things that have transpired since then that have brought their marriage to where it is now, the same is true today.

Ironically, Dr. Gottman and I are of one mind here. We both agree that the problem (conflict) cannot be resolved. Where we part company is in our response to this reality. I will take up Dr. Gottman's response first. I will then indicate mine in Chapter 23.

While Dr. Gottman talks in terms of "divorce proofing" a marriage, he acknowledges that it is not really possible to do that. As he says, "*most marital arguments cannot be solved. Couples spend year after year trying to change each other's mind—but it can't be done.*" (P. 28) But he really doesn't acknowledge the full implications of this. Rather, as is so often the case, he sidesteps the issue by falling back on his standard response when it comes to the problems that husbands and wives are having in their marriage. Thus, his recommendation is that "they need to understand the bottom-line difference that is causing the conflict—and to learn how to live with it *by honoring and respecting each other.*" (emphasis added) (P. 28) In my terms, he distracts our attention away from the problem and romanticizes it away by introducing the idea of *honoring and respecting each other.*

He does this in other distracting ways as well, in this case by falling back on what he characterizes as the "scientific studies" he conducted over a number of decades. Thus, he says,

> "I was not able to crack the code to saving marriages until I started to analyze what went *right* in happy marriages. After tracking the lives of happily married couples for as long as twenty years, I now know that the key to reviving or divorce proofing a relationship is not simply how you handle your disagreements but how you engage with one another when you're are not fighting. So . . . the basis of my approach . . . is to strengthen the friendship and trust that are at the heart of any marriage . . . . Bolstering your friendship is so critical in large part because it fuels the romance, passion, and great sex that we all hope marriage will provide." (P. 51)

III

This brings us to the critical question. Dr. Gottman acknowledges that, like so many mental health professionals before him, he had gotten it wrong. As he says, "At first, when I figured out how to predict divorce, I thought that I had found the key to saving marriages." (P. 51) But, as he later acknowledged, he was wrong.

But predicting a divorce is not the issue, and the grand introduction to his book, where he points to the study that he conducted of 130 newlywed couples, and his prediction as to who amongst them would end up divorcing over the next seven years, was simply a distraction. Couples who seek his help do not come to him to have him predict whether or not they will divorce. They come to him to have him predict whether or not he will be able to help them sustain their marriage. That, so he claims, is what his years of scientific research has taught him how to do.

Before I turn to that question, however, I want to go back to the study of the 130 newlywed couples that he conducted. Did he really predict which of them would end up getting divorced? He knew that approximately one half of them, or 65, would. (P. 3) The only question, therefore, was who amongst them would be one of those 65. We now knew that 17 would do so before the seven year period ended, fifteen of whose divorces he accurately predicted. But before I get to his prediction when it came to 15 of that 17, I want to address the remaining 48.

What prediction did Dr. Gottman make when it came to those 48. He didn't make any. He couldn't possibly have. He listened to them interact with one another for only 15 minutes and there wasn't anything in their interaction during that 15 minute period that could have told him one way or the other.

But that was obviously not the end of the story. Their marriage was going to go on, and when it did something was going to happen that would lead to their divorce. It could be the death of a child, financial reverses, a severe illness, or just the fact that what was now a small problem developed into a much larger one. Obviously, Dr. Gottman could not know this, which was why he could not make any prediction as to which of them would end up divorcing. But there was something else that he could not know which would bear upon this, and that was whether or not they would seek professional help if and when a problem developed in their marriage and how effective or ineffective it would be in helping them sustain their marriage.

But who amongst the remaining 113 would be the ones who would divorce was not the issue. After all, as the title of Dr. Gottman's book proclaimed, what he was attempting to do was to provide them with a roadmap which, if they followed, would enable them to go the distance. That being the case, what someone who turned to Dr. Gottman for help wanted to know was if he could predict whether following the roadmap he was recommending would leave them, as he put it in the title of his book, with a marriage that works.

Dr. Gottman never got into that question. To be sure, he proclaimed how many of them would end up getting divorced. But he knew that in advance. It was about 50%. But he was completely silent when it came to the two central questions, namely, who of them would be amongst that 50% and, more important, what percentage of those 65 couples who sought his help with respect to the problems they were experiencing in their marriage would be left with a marriage that works—a marriage that goes the distance.

But he was also completely silent when it came to a third critical question. Even if his intervention was successful, how long would it take?

This is not an academic question. Nor is it one of no significance. As so many of the stories that I related in Part I underscored, over and over again couples who turned to mental health professionals for help with the problems they were having in their marriage found themselves on a merry-go ride that never seemed to end. I do not mean for a couple of weeks. I do not mean for a couple of months. In many instances it was for one or two years, and sometimes longer. Needless to say, that is unacceptable. So it is not sufficient for Dr, Gottman to tell a couple who comes to him for help what his success rate is. It is also necessary for him to tell them how long he believes it will take before he will know whether or not he will be successful in their case. I will return to this in the next chapter.

CHAPTER 22

THE SECOND ASSESSMENT

Two heads are better than one

Let us assume that you have decided to go back and attempt to address the problems in your marriage. If that is the case, the threshold question you have to answer is who are you going to turn to for help. Unfortunately, I can only be of limited help to you here in the sense that I cannot recommend someone to you. I do not even know what state, city or town you live in. Nevertheless, I think that I can be of some help to you when it comes to this critical question.

First. Plan to meet with two people rather than just one. It is a lot easier to compare two people than it is to make a judgment about just one person. Obviously, if you are not comfortable with either of the two, you can meet with a third.

Second. By definition you want someone who has read this book, endorses the understanding it is based on, and follows the roadmap it recommends. If you have been persuaded by what I have said, why would you select someone who does not endorse that understanding and follow that roadmap?

Third. I do not think that it makes any difference whether the person you choose is a man or a woman. But that does not mean that it may not make a difference to one of you. Since it is important that you both feel comfortable with the person you will be working with, if one of you would prefer to work with a woman rather than a man, or visa-versa, if the other does not have a problem with that, I think you should go with it. I am not suggesting that there may not be a man's perspective and a woman's perspective. I am already on record as having said that I believe that there is. Why, then, does this not concern me? Because if either of you come to feel that this is the case when it comes to the person you have selected, you can always terminate the counseling. In other words, whether the person you select will or will not be impartial is not your problem. It is his or her problem.

Fourth. I think that the person you choose should be a mental health professional. This does not mean that I believe that someone who is not a mental health professional might not qualify for the job. It is just that I think that someone who has had a lot of experience working with husbands and wives who were having problems in their marriage is a better choice. You will notice that I have not gotten into the educational background of the mental health professional in question. I will address that in a minute.

Fifth. Men and women may be interchangeable. But smart and not so smart people are not, and you are going to want the smartest person you can find. What the person in question will be embarking upon is not going to be a piece of cake. If it was, the two of you could have done this on your own. That is why you will want the smartest person you can find. I believe that, as a general rule, someone with a doctoral degree is smarter than someone with a master's degree. That is not because he (or she) has a doctoral degree rather than a master's degree. In most instances (but not all) it is the other way around. He has a doctoral degree rather than a master's degree because he is smarter.

Finally, pick someone who is both friendly and professional. As I like to say, you do not want someone who is so friendly that he ceases to be professional or so professional that he ceases to be friendly. Nevertheless, at the end of the day, professionalism is the most important.

I

There is a lot more to discuss when it comes to this second assessment. But I want to clear something up before I get into it. You have already conducted your own assessment. That was to determine whether you wished to go back and address the problems in your marriage and, based on what you learned about the problems you were confronted with from reading this book, whether you thought you would be successful if you did that. We will call that a subjective assessment. But you also want to have what I will label an objective assessment, one made by someone who has had a great deal of experience working with couples who, like you, were having serious problems in their marriage. If he (or she) has met the two of you, has come to know you, has gotten a sense of the problems you are having and, more important, how you relate to one another, based on his experience he should be able to make what I have referred to as an assessment as to whether or not it is realistic for you to believe that you have a good chance of successfully dealing with those problems. I said "good chance." Nothing is certain. Only time will tell.

Obviously, if he concludes that you do, you know what you will do. You have already made that decision. But suppose that is not his conclusion. Suppose, further, that you decide to continue to work on the problems in your marriage. Will I be upset if that is your decision? Will I say that you are making a mistake? No. I won't even know what decision you came to. But even if I did, I would not pass judgment. Who am I to do that. This is your life, not mine. That is not a casual statement on my part. It is a very important one.

Why am I telling you this? Because I do not want you to proceed worrying about the outcome of this second assessment. All that you are trying to do is get a more objective opinion when it comes to the problems you are faced with. What you do with that information is your business, not mine or the person conducting the assessment.

II

This brings me to the assessment itself. It is not going to take place when you first meet the mental health professional in question. When I was in practice, I used to refer to this as "a get to know you meeting." You haven't even decided to employ the person in question or he (or she) to take you on.

Let us assume that you have found someone who you feel comfortable with and he has agreed to work with you. If you have not done so, there are still some things that you have to attend to.

First. If you have sought professional help before, you must make it clear to the person you have selected that you do not want to make a career of this, going from one mental health professional to another. You are willing to attribute your failure in the past to the fact that the mental health professional you were working with was following the wrong roadmap. But as the person with whom you are now meeting has told you, he does not subscribe to that roadmap. He subscribes to the one advanced in this book.

Second. You appreciate that, because of the limited time that he spent with you at that first meeting, he may not have been in a position to tell you whether he thought you had a good chance of being able to sustain your marriage. But if you meet with him two or three more times, and particularly as he gets to know you better and how you interrelate with one another, he should be in a much better position to express an opinion.

Further, you know that it will take some time to get from where you are today to where you want to be. But since you are both very anxious to sustain your marriage, if he feels that you are making progress, you will have no problem investing more time. But if, based on the assessment that he will later make, he does not feel confident that you will be successful, you will expect him to tell you that so you will be able to make a second assessment for yourself. In other words, as you have put your cards on the table with him, you expect him to put his cards on the table with you. Remember, you are meeting with him in order to get to know him and to make an assessment of him as well. If you sought professional help in the past, you were not in a position to do that. Having read this book, you should now be better able to do that.

This is critical. As the numerous examples I gave of the couples who turned to mental health professionals for help with the problems they were experiencing in their marriage, how long they stayed in counselling before they just gave in and gave up, and how many times they then turned to a different mental health professional only to end up no better off, there is only one conclusion that can be drawn from that. And that is that they deserved far better from those the mental health professionals they turned to for help than to be left with the merry-go-round ride going nowhere that they were given.

Why do I describe it as a merry-go-round ride? If Dr. Gottman claims that a competent mental health professional should be able to predict whether a married couple will or will not divorce in the next seven years by observing them interact with one another for only 15 minutes, that same mental health professional should be able to conclude that he (or she) will or will not be able to help them sustain their marriage if he has had an opportunity to meet with them two or three times, in each instance for an hour. After all, this is marriage counseling not rocket science, and you are not the first couple who he has counselled.

But the sad fact is that, with rare exception, a mental health professional who follows the current roadmap does not make such an assessment. Dr. Gottman never suggested that he did. He (or she) will just sit there and listen to the couple in question for as long as they are willing to come in and meet with him. It is the couple, and not he, who will end up making that assessment and terminate the therapy. As I said, you deserve better than that.

That is why I have built this second assessment into the new roadmap I am proposing. That is also why I made a point of the fact that Dr. Gottman never disclosed in his book what his success rate was when it came to those couples who came to him for help. If that is the case, why have I not built into my new roadmap the suggestion that, in interviewing a mental health professional, you should ask him (or her) the question that Dr. Gottman never answered, namely, what is his success rate? Because it is irrelevant. You are not interested in his success rate with other couples he has worked with in the past. You are interested in what he thinks his chances will be in your case.

CHAPTER 23

ACCEPTING THE LIMITATIONS IN THE UNDERTAKING

One Cannot Expect Perfect Solutions To Imperfect Problems

If the therapeutic intervention you plan to engage in is going to be successful, it is important that you know what you have a right to expect and not expect.

I appreciate that what you expect is to be able to solve the problems you are confronted with in your marriage. After all, why else have you decided to turn for help?

I need to disabuse you of that expectation. There is only one sure way to solve the problems that you are having in your marriage and that is to go forward, get a divorce, and end your marriage. After all, isn't it correct to say that your problem is the fact that you are married?

Why am I telling you this? For two reasons. First, because I want to be straight with you. I make no pretense of the fact that I want you to trust me and to follow my advice. In that regard, I like to think that my insight, understanding and sound judgment are the most important things that I can give to you. Second, because I want to act as a reality principle.

There are things in the life that we lead that we have control over and things that we do not. Needless to say, if the success of something you are undertaking is dependent upon your changing the things that you do not have any control over, you are destined to fail. Thus, while you could no doubt lose ten pounds, you could not grow two inches, and if sustaining your marriage is dependent on that, you are not going to succeed. In the context here, there are things that you can improve and things that you cannot.

And that is the problem. It is also the challenge. I do not want to get into all of the things that you cannot change or improve, such as your in-laws or other members of you family, or the fact that you have to work to make a living. As we say, they come with the territory. Besides, in most instances (such as having to work to make a living) they are either not really a problem or one that you have found a way to live with.

But there are two things that are undermining your ability to sustain your marriage which you cannot change. I have already underscored them. That is the fact that the two of you have very different emotional dispositions and very different adaptive styles and that they clash with one another. Why do you have so little control over them? Because, as is the case with other things that constitute who you are, they are in your DNA. The only difference is that most of those other things do not constitute a problem in your marriage. These two do.

This was brought home to me when I read another book of Dr. Gottman's where he referred to the fact that husbands and wives very often had very different styles when it came to dealing with problems in their marriage, in this case the wife wanting to put the problem on the table and deal with it, the husband not wanting to do that. That is not how I read the situation. It was not attributable to their having different styles in dealing with problems in their marriage. From the wife's point of view, her husband was not dealing with the problem. From the husband's point of view, his wife was creating a problem where there was none.

The point (and only point) is that you were never going to convince the wife here that there wasn't a problem or the husband that there was. Contrary to what Dr. Guttman suggested, this had nothing to do with whether or not there really was a problem. It had to do with the fact that their adaptive strategies were such that the wife saw everything (or almost everything) as being a problem and that the husband saw nothing (or almost nothing) as being a problem. Again, they were not going to get anywhere debating whether there was or was not a problem. If the therapeutic intervention was going to be effective at all, it would have to be directed at the fact that the wife's adaptive style tended to create problems and the husband's adaptive style tended to ignore them and to get them to see this.

I have to acknowledge that I have over simplified the issue. The issue isn't just whether there is or is not a problem. The issue is also how the two of you should deal with it, and as with the problem itself, you are not going to be of one mind here. Again, that is a function of the fact that the two of you come to your marriage with very different emotional dispositions and adaptive styles and that they clash with one another. And since you can't change the reality of your different emotional dispositions or adaptive styles, it is not possible to solve the problem they have left you with. What then is the answer?

I like to think that I have told you many things that will be of help to you if you have decided to go back and get help in an effort to sustain your marriage—that you understand the problems you are experiencing in your marriage a little better now than you did when you first picked up this book. But if you come away remembering only one thing I have told you, what I am now going to tell you should be that one thing.

It is not possible for you to solve this problem. As I said at the beginning of this chapter, you cannot expect perfect solutions to imperfect problems. That is because, while there are some things that you can change, like losing 10 pounds, there are other things that you cannot change, like growing two inches.

But the fact that you cannot solve a problem doesn't necessarily mean that you cannot deal with it—in the terms that I will put it, "beat it." Let me explain. The fact that you will not be able to solve the problem that your different emotional dispositions and adaptive styles have created in your marriage will no doubt mess up your hair a bit–create a little *sturm und drang* (storm and stress) in your lives. As they say, that comes with the territory—they are inherent in your relationship. But the fact that you cannot solve that problem doesn't necessarily mean that you cannot beat it. How can you do that? By resolving that you will never let it beat you. By understanding the problem a little better—in the context here, understanding that you will never be able to solve it. All that you can do is beat it by learning to live with it.

Will that alone enable you to do that? I didn't say that. Except for death, nothing in life is certain. But that resolve will hopefully give you an advantage that you have not had before—the fact that you have decided that you will be damned if you will ever let the problem beat you.

But you will need something else besides that determination. Although I did not put it in quite these terms, I already told you what it is at both the end of Chapter 12 and in Chapter 19, when you made the first assessment. I will now refer to it as separating the wheat from the chaff.

What I said there was that the necessary pre-condition for your decision to go back and get help in your effort to sustain your marriage was your belief that you are married to a basically decent person. Otherwise, what would you be left with if you were able to sustain your marriage? To put it another way, while your different emotional dispositions and adaptive styles are driving a wedge between the two of you, hopefully the fact that you both feel that you are married to a basically decent person will serve to strengthen your resolve to beat the problem you are faced with rather than allow it to beat you and, in doing that, increase your chances of success.

Is what I am suggesting just a mind game? Of course it is. So what if it gives you a far better chance of beating the problem than the romantic mind game that Dr. Gottman is recommending. That is what I mean when I say that the roadmap I am proposing is a far better one than the current one.

There is one last thing that has to be said when it comes to this new roadmap. It dramatically changes the name of the game and, with it, the role of the mental health professional to whom you will turn to for help.

You are going to be meeting with him on a regular basis, perhaps once a week in the beginning and less often thereafter. As I said, the purpose of those meeting is not to help you solve the problem. It is to help you beat it. That being the case, his role will be very different. Rather than being the principal player in the drama, he is going to coach the drama from the sidelines. When the two of you meet with him, he will get a sense of how well you are doing or not doing in your effort to beat the problem. Is it still on top of you or are you getting on top of it? That is where his new role as coach will come in. If you are doing pretty well on your own, he may just sit there and observe how you are doing. However, if it is clear that the problem is still getting the best of you, he will step in and coach you a little in an effort to maintain your resolve. Finally, if he concludes that you are not going to be able to beat the problem, he will tell you that as well. Since you do not want the problem to beat you, that may help you to maintain your resolve. If it does not, and since he has given you his assurance that he will not leave you on a merry-go ride going nowhere, he will honor his obligation to you and conclude the therapy.

CHAPTER 24

CONCLUSION

We are always required to make the decisions in
our lives with less than adequate information

The central premise of this book has been that the reason why mental health professionals have been less successful in helping husbands and wives work on the problems in their marriage than they could have been, and would have liked to be, was that they were following the wrong roadmap. In the terms that I put it, they were looking at the presenting problems rather than their cause. To understand their cause, so I argued, it was necessary to go back and look at what took place between them before they got married. That is when the seeds that eventually took root and undermined their marriage were planted.

I have not cited any authority for this. It is just a conclusion I came to on my own. As I said, I came to believe that husbands and wives commonly divorced one another for the very reasons that they married one another. As I put it, what had once been the mighty glue that held their relationship together had now become the acid that was eating it away.

Ironically, and after I completed the first draft of Part I, I came across an article, again in the Styles Section of *The New York Times*, entitled "Unhitched" by Louise Rafkin, that said very much the same thing. The author did not express it in the terms that I have. She didn't think in those terms. But it was nevertheless implicit in the story she told. I therefore want to relate it.

The couple here had married when they were 27 and 28 years of age, respectively, had two children together and divorced after 30 years, when their children were adults.

It didn't take too long before problems began to develop in their marriage. As the husband said, "I think we both resented each other for our differences." "In retrospect, we may have been in love with the idea of each other as opposed to who we really were." "I was angry at myself for marrying a romantic idea," she added.

"After seven years, they started couple therapy and went for many years to various counsellors, while also seeing individual therapists. Looking back after 30 years, she felt that they had had the same argument for 23 years." 'Nothing changed, and I'm not sure why not' she said. 'The counselors didn't make it clear what the problems really were'."

This, of course, had been my experience. In more instances than not, the couples who came to me to get divorced had turned to mental health professionals for help (often more than one) with the problems they were having in their marriage. And, as with the couple here, they had not been able to help them. It is not without significance how the wife here expressed that. "They hadn't made it clear enough what the problems really were." In my terms, how could they when they were following the wrong roadmap?

Ironically, though he wasn't using any roadmap at all, the husband saw what the problem was. To be sure, he had not been able to see it while they were married. He was too close to it to see it clearly and, like his wife, just got caught up in their arguments. But he was better able to see it now. As he said, "I'm not a planner and she's a hyper-planner. Its why we got together and why we fell apart." He was saying the same thing that I had been saying for years. Husbands and wives commonly divorced one another for the very reasons that they married one another.

But the story this couple told went even further. It also reinforced my thesis that we don't have one marriage. We have successive marriages, and the considerations that are at play operate more powerfully or less powerfully in each one of those successive marriages—for example, when the children are young and when they are older. As the wife said, "Kids are a wonderful distraction, but at some point that project is done and we couldn't agree on the next one."

To be sure, not viewing the problem in my terms, the wife didn't express it as I did. But since we were really saying the same thing, it is easy enough to translate what she said into my suggestion that we have successive marriages. What are children distracting us from? From the considerations that are undermining our marriage. At this stage in our marriage we don't want those considerations to get so out of hand as to jeopardize our marriage. It would cause too much harm to our children. But the situation is different once "that project is done" and we move on to the next of our successive marriages. Giving those considerations freer license then hopefully won't have the same effect.

I

Before I go on, I want to relate the story of two more marriages that Louise Rafkin wrote about in another issue of "Unhitched." I am doing this for a reason. The conclusions that I came to, and summed up in Chapter 18, were conclusions that I came to on the basis of both my own experience working in this field and from the wedding announcements that I read in the Styles Section of *The New York Times*. But those conclusions were not scientific facts, and other witnesses might have drawn different conclusions. Thus, I am relating the story of these two marriages that Louise Rafkin wrote about, just as I did the story of the first marriage, because they tend to confirm my own conclusion.

The husband in the first of these two stories was 25 and the wife 23 when they married. They met at a bar in San Francisco. "They had instant chemistry . . . Less than an hour later Mr. . . . announced his intention to marry her." For her part, she "never felt awkward or shy with (him), which she did with other men. He was handsome, smart, capable and charismatic." "My head was spinning. I was so in love with him," she said. After 26 years of marriage she filed for divorce. ". . . . is still my best friend" she said. "We joke that if we are not married by our 30th anniversary, maybe we should get back together again" he said.

The couple in the second of these stories met when she auditioned to play in his jazz band. He was a freelance television producer and she a neurologist. "A quirky, witty, goofy doctor who played great keyboard in a cute miniskirt. I was in awe of her brain power and immediately smitten" he said. "He stripped off his shirt during the rehearsal", which she found "crazy in a funny way." She ditched a then boyfriend and they were together all of the time.

"Initially they didn't want to divorce, but their problems—money, communication and a lack of appreciation for each other—persisted even though they saw several therapists for several years." They divorced after 15 years of marriage. "We did the best we could, but love blinds you to behavior that might put the marriage at risk" she said. "When the romantic and sexual haze goes away— and it always does—marriage becomes a project that takes rigorous honesty," he said.

II

I now want to return to the initial story of Louise Rafkin which I related. That story raises a second question. The couple there held out for 23 more years after they first sought professional help. As the wife put it, "She felt like they had had the same argument for 23 years." Would they have been better off if they had gotten a divorce 23 years earlier? The wife was now 60 and her husband 61. Wouldn't they have had more opportunities then than they have now? To be sure, it would have been more traumatic for their children, who were much younger then. But as they acknowledged, their children were still upset by their divorce even when they postponed it. Besides, who is to say what effect their 23 years of arguing had on their children. The wife's parents, who stayed married forever, apparently argued all of the time. What effect had that had on her?

I don't want to answer this question now. Rather, I want to pose another one. If the Husband and wife here had consulted with a mental health professional who followed the roadmap I am proposing, would they have been able to work on the problems in their marriage successfully? There was not enough in the article to answer that question. But there was enough to suggest that it might have made sense to try.

I got the sense that the husband and wife here were basically decent people. I also got the sense that, in talking to third parties, they each would have said complementary, rather than uncomplimentary, things about the other. They still had feelings for one another. This was evidenced by something the wife said. "He is family and the father to my children. I would do whatever I could for him without sacrificing my own integrity." In terms of my assessment, the two considerations that I referred to in the last chapter, together with their awareness that they each brought the problem with them to the marriage, are the most important in terms of assessing whether or not it might make sense for them to go back and work on the problems in their marriage rather than go forward, get a divorce and end it. Certainly that was the case when they entered therapy.

But there is another reason as well. Following the roadmap that I am proposing they substitute for the one they used in the past, what would they have had to lose if they were inclined to get help with the problems in their marriage? They would not have been committing themselves to years and years of therapy going nowhere. The mental health professional they decided to work with, who was in a far better position than either of them to do this, was going to make his or her own assessment as to whether or not it was realistic for them to believe that they would be able to make the accommodations necessary to leave them with a viable marriage—in my terms, one that met their essential needs. To be sure, if the answer to that question was yes, there would still be work to be done, and that would take time. But they would view that investment in time differently if they felt they were making progress rather than just going round in circles.

Let me now return to the question that I did not answer before. Would the two of them have been better off if they had gotten divorced 23 years earlier? In my terms, they made the assessment and, whether correctly or incorrectly, decided that they should go forward, get a divorce and end their marriage. I said "correctly or incorrectly" because we can't say "if they knew then what they know now." They couldn't have known then what they know now. That is why they could be making a mistake. As I said, if they decide to go back and work on the problems in their marriage, they will know whether or not they made a mistake. Moreover they will know that in a relatively short period of time. However, if they decide to go forward, get a divorce and end their marriage, they will never know.

This objection misses the essential point. The problem isn't, as I put it, whether they should go forward or they should go back. The problem is that they are not able to make that decision, as a result of which they are just aimlessly drifting, going nowhere. In my terms, the problem is that they are stuck. They are unable to hold on but, at the same time, they are unable to let go. So the choice is not between going forward or going back. It is between going forward, going back, or going nowhere—remaining stuck. And when it comes to all three of those choices, the last is the worst.

That is why it doesn't make sense for the two of them to beat themselves up by asking whether or not they would be making a mistake if they went forward, got a divorce and ended their marriage. Rather, as in life generally, it makes more sense to accept the limitations of the undertaking and make a decision rather than just drift, going nowhere. As I said, one cannot expect perfect solutions to imperfect problems.

But it goes beyond that. As I said, in most instances in the lives that we lead, we are forced to make decisions with less than adequate information. Ironically, this is one of the few exceptions to that. The wife here, who was the one who made the decision to divorce, didn't know more after 30 years of marriage than she did after 20 years of marriage. She didn't know more after 20 years than she knew after 10, or more after 10 than she did after 7, when they first went into marriage counselling. On the contrary, she knew all that she was going to know or needed to know then, and 23 more years of arguments didn't add anything. Thus, her problem wasn't a lack of sufficient information. Her problem was her inability to act on it. Her problem was that she was stuck—as I said, she was unable to hold on but also unable to let go.

CHAPTER 25

A FRESH START

If you do the same thing in the same way,
you will end up with the same result.

I want you to go back and imagine that it is a month before your wedding. If you had read this book, particularly the summary which I gave in Chapter 18, what would you do? Given what I have said up to this point, it would be natural to assume that if you had any sense you would call off the wedding. Now that you know what you are buying into, and that the odds are little better than fifty-fifty that the marriage will go the distance, how could you possibly take that chance. Even if you are amongst the lucky fifty percent, that only tells you that your marriage will not end in divorce. It doesn't tell you whether or not it will be a happy one. More important, if you had called off the wedding, you wouldn't be faced with the decision with which you are now faced.

I appreciate the fact that you have to assume that I would concur in that decision. After all, I am hardly a fan of romantic marriage. In fact, I agree with Freud that falling in love is akin to a mental illness.

But I am not going to suggest that you do that. Let us consider the situation. If you call off the wedding, it will not be because you have decided to withdraw from this world and enter a monastery or nunnery. It will be because you have doubts about the prospects of your forthcoming marriage. In part at least that will be because reading this book has made you realize that you really do not know that much about your future husband or wife, that your common interests are not as important as you thought they were and, most important, that the powerful feelings that now so overwhelm you, which are at best only short lived, are really no indication of how this will all turn out.

Where will that leave you? Obviously, nowhere. You will just be at square one again. Where do you go from there? You could go into an arranged marriage, perhaps one arranged by your parents. After all, that was how many men and women got married in the past. For all we know, that may be how they will get married in the not too distant future. But that is not how they get married today. So if you call off your wedding, you will not do that. Rather, you will just go and wait for lightening to strike again. In other word, you will end up exactly where you are now.

But there is another alternative. Start dating again. The only requirement is that you select someone who is cut from the same cloth as you are. By "the same cloth" I do not mean someone of the same sex, the same race, the same religious background or even someone who has the same level of formal education. I only mean someone who fits in with your friends. Start spending time with that person. Remember, you are not waiting for lightning to strike. You are only trying to get to know them better. Thus the test is not whether you are in love with them. It is whether you like them—whether you feel comfortable with them and whether they are a basically decent person. You are waiting to see whether affection develops between the two you, not whether you fall madly in love with them. Toward that end, do not rush to get into bed with them. Sex should be an extension of affection not an independent activity that has nothing to do with affection. That is what whore houses are for.

I appreciate the fact that what I have just said sounds like the expression of a moral judgment on my part. It isn't. There is a difference between moral judgments and a value system. There is also a difference between moral judgments and rational judgments, and as the many examples that I cited in Chapter 10 should have made clear, there is currently very little rationality involved when it comes to what is probably the most important decision that anyone will make in his or her life. If that is the case, it doesn't make sense to load the dice and increase that risk by employing a procedure that you don't need more than your common sense to tell you is nothing short of irrational.

Suppose you follow my suggestion when it comes to how you will meet someone new and form a relationship with them. Suppose further that you come to like the person, and being with them, very much. Suppose as well that you enjoy having intimate sexual relations with them. But also suppose that you are not in love with them—that you have not been swept off your feet. What should you do. Marry them if they will have you.

I

Is that what I am suggesting you should do? Yes and no. To be sure, I think that I have given you very good advice. Unfortunately, it is not that simple. Let me start with why the answer is no.

There are two reasons for this. The first is that you are not going to follow my suggestion, which is why it is a waste of time. I admit that sounds like a criticism. It isn't, and I do not want you to be hard on yourself if you don't. I am more interested in your following the spirit of what I suggested rather than that you view it as being the letter of the law. You were born at a different time and place than were those who married 300 or 400 years ago. It is unrealistic to believe that the same values and influences that dictated when and who men and women married then will have any influence on who you will marry today. How could they when you live in a totally different world than they did?

This brings me to the second problem. Even if you did follow my advice to the letter of the law by not allowing yourself to be carried away by the mandates of romantic love, that does not mean that you will not have problems in your marriage. It doesn't even guarantee that you may not be in the very large group of people whose marriages do not go the distance. That is because, if you have read this book carefully, you know that there are a whole array of considerations other than the fantasy of romantic love that can undermine your marriage, principally your different emotional dispositions and adaptive styles.

But, having read this book, won't you be far more aware of your different emotional dispositions and adaptive styles, and how they run interference with one another, than was previously the case? The answer is no. As I pointed out earlier, the two of you are going to conduct your relationship on a very narrow playing field, one on which your different emotional dispositions and adaptive styles will not be prominently displayed. But won't that be deceptive on your part. No. You won't even be aware of it. As I said, it will be all smiles, hugs and kisses. After all, even if you are persuaded by everything that I have said in this book, that doesn't mean that you and the person you are involved with will not have intimate sexual relations? Nor does it mean that you will highlight your different personal dispositions and adaptive styles.

That is why the answer to the question as to whether you should follow my advice to the letter of the law is no. But, as I said, it is also yes. Not to the letter of the law, but to its spirit.

Having read this book, you hopefully now have a much better understanding than you previously did as to the considerations which today induces men and women to make the leap of faith involved in their decision to marry. I refer to it as a leap of faith because it is not possible for there to have been any rational basis for their decisions. How could there have been when they were induced to make that decision based on a fantasy? Thus, you owe it to yourself to attempt to make that decision more thoughtfully.

Having said that, I want to acknowledge that it will not be possible for you to do that completely, any more than it is realistic to believe that the two of you will postpone having intimate sexual relations until after you have married. That is just not the world that we live in today. But it doesn't have to be all or nothing. That is the distinction I made between following the letter of the law and following the spirit of what I am saying. But you cannot afford to completely ignore it, as we do today. There is just too much riding on it.

II

I said earlier that I had no dog in this fight-—that I was not trying to persuade you to go in one direction or the other. However, in the name of full disclosure, I must add one thing. In Chapter 16, I indicated all of the changes that had taken place in society in the last several centuries that have had the effect of both changing our attitude toward marriage and undermining the social props which previously tended to support it, to the point that nearly one-half of all first marriages in the United States today end in divorce, and that what we have been left with is "serial monogamy."

Unlike those on the political and religious right, I do now view marriage in religious terms or as being inviolate. I also view their belief that the reason that marriage is in the state that it is today is that it has been invaded from the outside by a moral virus, and that all that it is necessary to restore it to its previous state is to give it a moral shot in the arm, to be more than naive and simplistic. The historical and social changes that I outlined in that chapter have irrevocably changed life as we know it. We understand that when it comes to all of the other changes that have taken place in that time. To be sure, the introduction of the automobile has brought with it far more fatal traffic accidents. But is anyone on the political or religious right suggesting that we should go back to the horse and buggy?

In similar fashion, the historical and cultural changes that I outlined in that chapter have had a profound effect on our lives, and as every student of the family has acknowledged, ours is a far more anonymous, impersonal, individualistic and hedonistic world than it was just a few centuries ago, and this has affected every aspect of our lives. And it was these developments and, particularly, the introduction of the idea of romantic marriage, that undermined marriage as we knew it little more than a century ago.

Having said that (and this is where the full disclosure comes in), I believe that, for the very reasons that it has been undermined, marriage is more important today than it has ever been before. We derive satisfaction and meaning in our lives from two sources, our work and the close personal relationships that we form, particularly with the immediate members of our family. For those of us who are lucky (and we are in the minority), we derive that satisfaction from both of those sources in equal measure. That is when our work is interesting and intellectually challenging, or we have the sense that we are building something or doing something that is of value. The same is not true for the vast majority of us, however. Work is just what we do to make a living. To be sure, work has always been drudgery for the vast majority of mankind. But people's expectations were much lower then. The historical and cultural forces that have brought us to where we are today have changed all of that. That, as we saw, was implicit in the fact that we live in a far more secular world. It means that we look to this world rather than to the next one for meaning and fulfillment in our lives.

As I said earlier, when we lived in a rural society, the world of work and the world of our personal relations were one. The industrial revolution changed all of that. Those two worlds are now separate. To be sure, we have been brought up to function effectively in that larger, outer world. But increasingly, and in an important sense, that outer world has become unreal, and one over which we have little if any real control. (How often have you heard it said that politics is just a spectator sport?) That being the case, many if not most of us feel that we are entering the real world when we leave work and go home to our husband or wife, and to our children.

Children, of course, are important for many reasons. It is something that we participate in together. In most cases, it is not something that we each separately bring to the marriage. It is something that we create in the marriage. Better still, it is hopefully something that we are both invested in and in the name of which we are willing to subordinate our individual interests.

But, as I previously noted, our lives with our children is time limited. They grow up, move out, and build new lives for themselves, often some distance away. Then it is just the two of us. Moreover, given our dramatically increased life expectancies in the last 60 or 70 years, we can expect that our marriage beyond that point may be almost as long, and perhaps even longer, than it was before. As I said, health issues aside, many happily married couples will tell you that this is the best time of their lives—because they have one another. In an impersonal and anonymous world, it is very nice to have someone there who cares for you.

That is why I believe it is so unfortunate that, at the very time when we need the structure and stability that marriage has the possibility of providing more than ever before, it has become so much more difficult to maintain. (To complete my full disclosure, I have only been married once, and for over 50 years. I am telling you this because I do not want you to conclude from the fact that I have spent almost my entire professional life working in the field of divorce, have written more books on the subject than perhaps anyone else in the world, and have an admittedly secular attitude when it comes to marriage, that I have a cavalier attitude toward it. Nothing could be further from the truth.)

Having said that, it is necessary to add one thing. If the relationship that we are talking about is to serve its increasingly important function, we are going to have to be more realistic in terms of what we can expect and not expect of it. As I said, this is the principal message of this book. To be sure, the fantasies and illusions that we have allowed to overwhelm our decision making processes are without question very intoxicating. But they are also nothing but fool's gold, as everyone who gets taken in by them learns all too quickly. And none of us can afford to be a fool in a matter as important as this.

Is there enough left in the relationship without the intoxication that these fantasies and illusions afford us? In a way, that is an irrelevant question, For better or worse, that is all that we are going to be left with. But the answer is yes. As I said, in the increasingly anonymous and impersonal world in which we live, it is very nice to have someone there who cares for us. But if it is to serve that purpose, we are going to have to do two things. The first is to accept the fact that we are going to lead separate, parallel lives that come together and then separate over time, rather than one seamless life together. In the terms that I have put it, we are going to have to substitute the roadmap I am proposing for the one we have employed in the past. The second is that we are going to have to be willing and able to choose who it is that we form these relationships with on a more realistic basis. In my terms. we are going to have to make the assessment that I have called for before we get married. To be sure, that will not eliminate all of the problems. As I pointed out in Chapter 16, the considerations that will later become problems in the marriage come from a number of different sources, not just one, and they play out in different ways. The first, which I concentrated on most, was our romantic vision of marriage, which introduced the most irrational considerations that now affect the decision making process. The second is that we are going to have to be able and willing to choose who it is that we form these relations with on a more realistic basis. To be sure, that will not eliminate all of the risks. But, hopefully, it may diminish them.

I appreciate that my attitude toward marriage doesn't sound very romantic. But I would take strong exception to that. If you need proof here, just ask any couple who has been married for thirty years or more, who would describe their marriage as a happy one, and you will have all of the proof that you need.

This is my counsel to you. Without question, there will be others whose counsel will be different than mine. In fact, many of them will take strong exception to what I am saying. They will say that I do not have a very high regard for marriage. They may even accuse me of encouraging you to end yours. If you believe that, you haven't read this book very carefully.

As I purposely said, I have only been married once and for more than 50 years. I also strongly endorse Christopher Lash's suggestion that marriage is probably more important today than it has ever been in the past. To be sure, I am not a big fan of romantic love, any more than I am of any other hallucinatory drug. But that does not mean that I am recommending that you should pick your future husband's or wife's name out of a hat. As I said, you would still be faced with many of the same problems if you did. All that I am saying is that, whatever you choose to do, you should be more realistic when it comes to what you have and do not have a right to expect.

I will just close by adding one more thing. I believe that I have given you everything you need to know in terms of deciding what you are going to do, and that if you go back and read the book again you will see that. That is not the problem. The problem is acting on the decision, particularly if it is to go forward, get a divorce and end your marriage.

I like to think that I have made that decision a little bit easier as well. If you decide to go back and give it one last try, I am not suggesting that you should give it a year or two. That was the fate of all of those who followed the wrong road map. The road map that I have proposed insists that you will know everything that you need to know in no more than two to three months, and perhaps erven sooner. It will either happen or it won't happen, and if it hasn't happened in that time, it won't. I want to be clear here. I am not saying that if that is the case you should go forward, get a divorce and end your marriage. I don't make decisions in other people's lives. All I am saying is that you should make your decision with the understanding that if you decide not to divorce, all that you can expect is more of the same. If nothing has changed, nothing will change.

PART III

Ending the Marriage

CHAPTER 26

THE TWO DIFFERENT ROADMAPS

You have decided to go forward, get a divorce, and end your marriage. Regardless of whether that decision was made by one of you or by both of you, the problem you are now faced with is the same. How are you going to go about doing that? If the two of you have been married for a relatively short period of time, if you did not have children together, and if there has not been any significant change in your circumstances during your marriage, you may well be able to do this pretty much on your own. The court publishes forms that you can use for that purpose.

It will be very different, however, if that is not the case. Then you are going to need help. And, once again, there will be two very different roadmaps that you can follow when it comes to getting that help. Which one you chose will depend on the destination you want to come to. Obviously reading this book will not help you make that decision. But, as I said, I wrote a companion book to this one that will. It is entitled *A Common Sense, Practical Guide To Divorce*, and if you felt that this book was of help to you, I think you will find that that book will be as well.